NUKING ALASKA

NUKING ALASKA

NOTES OF AN ATOMIC FUGITIVE

PETER DUNLAP-SHOHL

graphic mundi

Library of congress cataloging-in-publication Data

Names: Dunlap-Shohl, Peter, 1958-- author.
Title: Nuking Alaska : notes of an atomic fugitive / Peter Dunlap-Shohl.
Description: University Park, Pennsylvania : Graphic Mundi, [2023] | Includes bibliographical references.
Summary: "An autobiographical account, in graphic novel format, of growing up in cold War Alaska in the shadow of a nuclear arsenal"--Provided by publisher.
Identifiers: LCCN 2022045721 | ISBN 9781637790472 (paperback)
Subjects: LCSH: Dunlap-Shohl, Peter, 1958---Comic books, strips, etc. | Cold War--Comic books, strips, etc. | Nuclear weapons--United States--Testing--Comic books, strips, etc. | Cannikin Project--Comic books, strips, etc. | Nuclear weapons--Testing--Environmental aspects--Comic books, strips, etc. | Alaska--History, Military--Comic books, strips, etc. | LCGFT: Graphic novels. | Environmental comics. | Autobiographical comics.
Classification: LCC F910 .D86 2023 | DDC 979.8/051--dc23/eng/20220928
LC record available at https://lccn.loc.gov/2022045721

Printed in China
Published by The Pennsylvania State University Press,
University Park, PA 16802--1003

10 9 8 7 6 5 4 3 2 1

graphic mundi
drawing our worlds together

Graphic Mundi is an imprint of The Pennsylvania State University Press.

The Pennsylvania State University Press is a member of the Association of University Presses.

It is the policy of The Pennsylvania State University Press to use acid-free paper. Publications on uncoated stock satisfy the minimum requirements of American National Standard for Information Sciences--Permanence of Paper for Printed Library Material, ANSI Z39.48--1992.

FOR WILEY

"I FEEL LIKE A FUGITIVE FROM THE LAW OF AVERAGES."
~ BILL MAULDIN

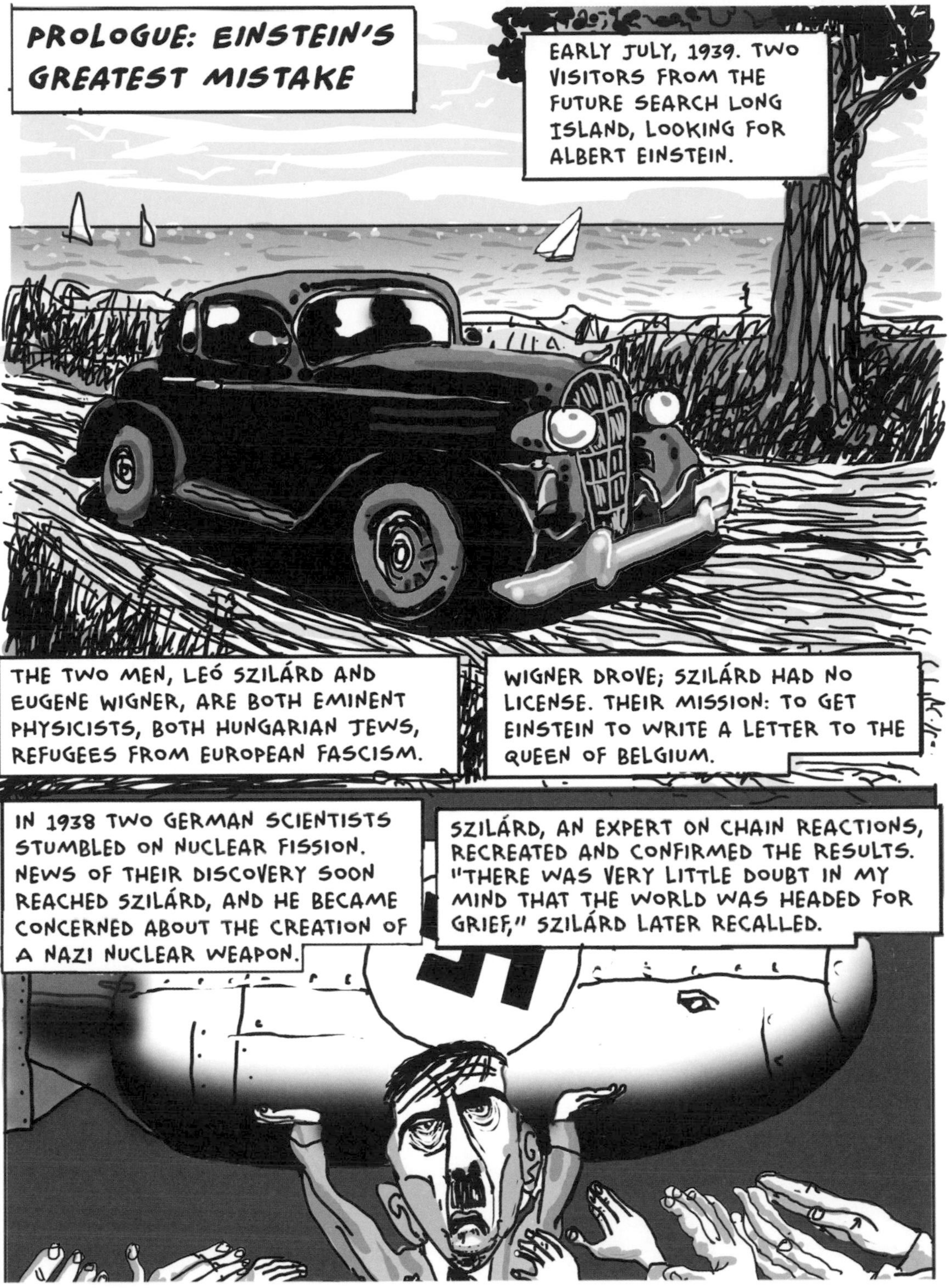
PROLOGUE: EINSTEIN'S GREATEST MISTAKE
EARLY JULY, 1939. TWO VISITORS FROM THE FUTURE SEARCH LONG ISLAND, LOOKING FOR ALBERT EINSTEIN.
THE TWO MEN, LEÓ SZILÁRD AND EUGENE WIGNER, ARE BOTH EMINENT PHYSICISTS, BOTH HUNGARIAN JEWS, REFUGEES FROM EUROPEAN FASCISM.
WIGNER DROVE; SZILÁRD HAD NO LICENSE. THEIR MISSION: TO GET EINSTEIN TO WRITE A LETTER TO THE QUEEN OF BELGIUM.
IN 1938 TWO GERMAN SCIENTISTS STUMBLED ON NUCLEAR FISSION. NEWS OF THEIR DISCOVERY SOON REACHED SZILÁRD, AND HE BECAME CONCERNED ABOUT THE CREATION OF A NAZI NUCLEAR WEAPON.
SZILÁRD, AN EXPERT ON CHAIN REACTIONS, RECREATED AND CONFIRMED THE RESULTS. "THERE WAS VERY LITTLE DOUBT IN MY MIND THAT THE WORLD WAS HEADED FOR GRIEF," SZILÁRD LATER RECALLED.

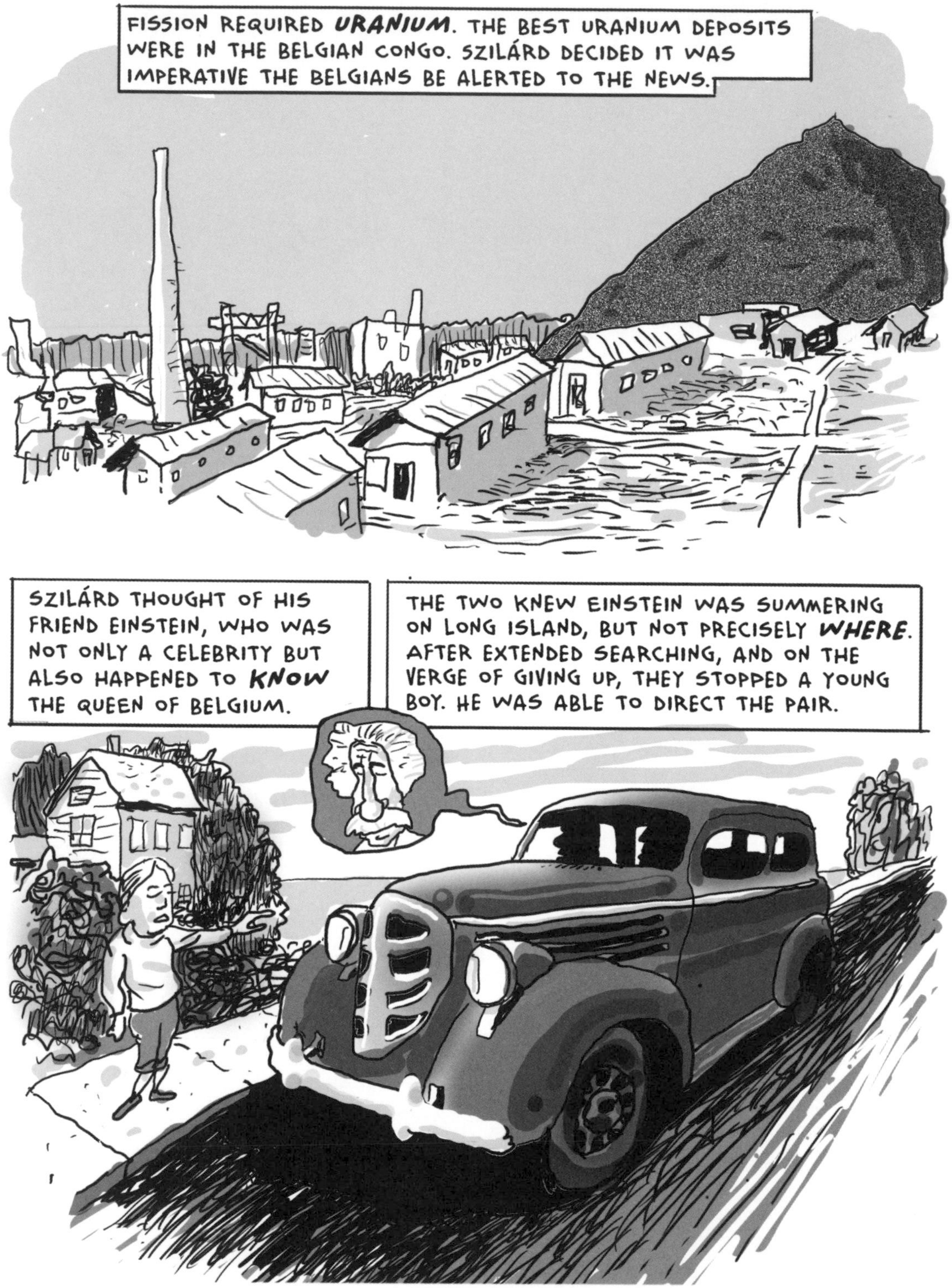
FISSION REQUIRED URANIUM. THE BEST URANIUM DEPOSITS WERE IN THE BELGIAN CONGO. SZILÁRD DECIDED IT WAS IMPERATIVE THE BELGIANS BE ALERTED TO THE NEWS.
SZILÁRD THOUGHT OF HIS FRIEND EINSTEIN, WHO WAS NOT ONLY A CELEBRITY BUT ALSO HAPPENED TO KNOW THE QUEEN OF BELGIUM.
THE TWO KNEW EINSTEIN WAS SUMMERING ON LONG ISLAND, BUT NOT PRECISELY WHERE. AFTER EXTENDED SEARCHING, AND ON THE VERGE OF GIVING UP, THEY STOPPED A YOUNG BOY. HE WAS ABLE TO DIRECT THE PAIR.

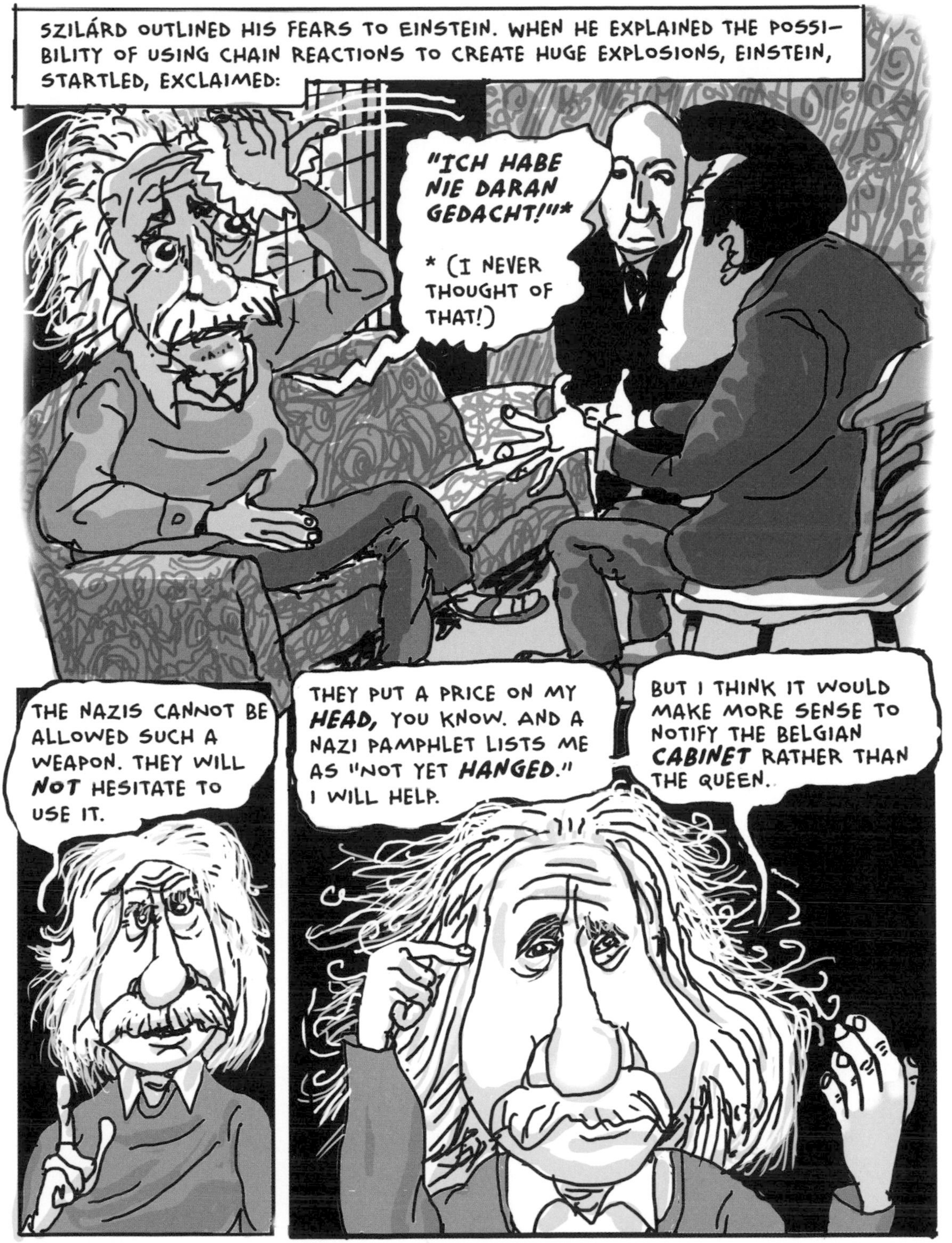
SZILÁRD OUTLINED HIS FEARS TO EINSTEIN. WHEN HE EXPLAINED THE POSSIBILITY OF USING CHAIN REACTIONS TO CREATE HUGE EXPLOSIONS, EINSTEIN, STARTLED, EXCLAIMED:
"ICH HABE NIE DARAN GEDACHT!"* * (I NEVER THOUGHT OF THAT!)
THE NAZIS CANNOT BE ALLOWED SUCH A WEAPON. THEY WILL NOT HESITATE TO USE IT.
THEY PUT A PRICE ON MY HEAD, YOU KNOW. AND A NAZI PAMPHLET LISTS ME AS "NOT YET HANGED." I WILL HELP.
BUT I THINK IT WOULD MAKE MORE SENSE TO NOTIFY THE BELGIAN CABINET RATHER THAN THE QUEEN.

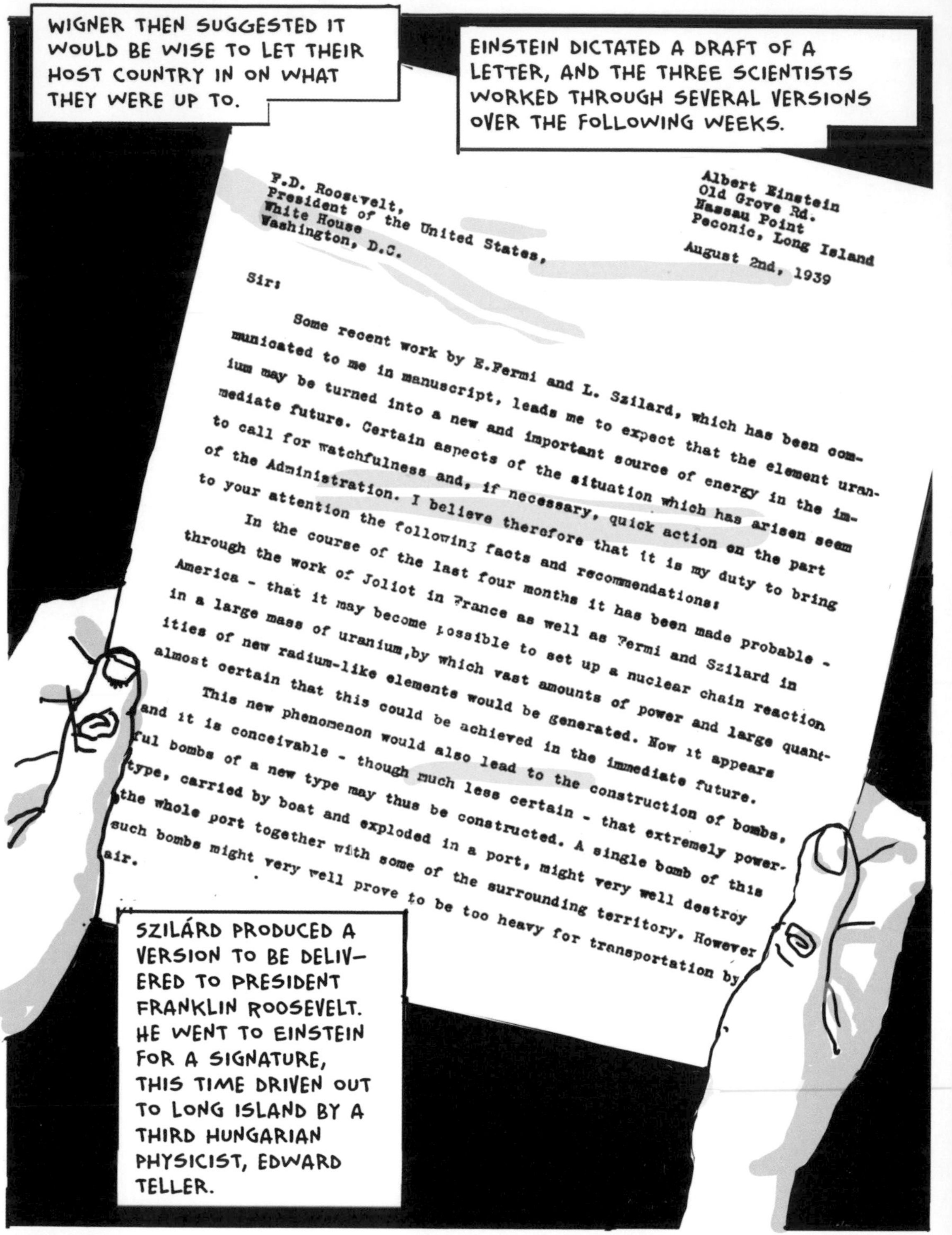

WIGNER THEN SUGGESTED IT WOULD BE WISE TO LET THEIR HOST COUNTRY IN ON WHAT THEY WERE UP TO.
EINSTEIN DICTATED A DRAFT OF A LETTER, AND THE THREE SCIENTISTS WORKED THROUGH SEVERAL VERSIONS OVER THE FOLLOWING WEEKS.
F.D. Roosevelt,
President of the United States,
White House
Washington, D.C.
Albert Einstein
Old Grove Rd.
Nassau Point
Peconic, Long Island
August 2nd, 1939
Sir:
Some recent work by E.Fermi and L. Szilard, which has been com-
municated to me in manuscript, leads me to expect that the element uran-
ium may be turned into a new and important source of energy in the im-
mediate future. Certain aspects of the situation which has arisen seem
to call for watchfulness and, if necessary, quick action on the part
of the Administration. I believe therefore that it is my duty to bring
to your attention the following facts and recommendations:
In the course of the last four months it has been made probable -
through the work of Joliot in France as well as Fermi and Szilard in
America - that it may become possible to set up a nuclear chain reaction
in a large mass of uranium,by which vast amounts of power and large quant-
ities of new radium-like elements would be generated. Now it appears
almost certain that this could be achieved in the immediate future.
This new phenomenon would also lead to the construction of bombs,
and it is conceivable - though much less certain - that extremely powerful bombs of a new type may thus be constructed. A single bomb of this
type, carried by boat and exploded in a port, might very well destroy
the whole port together with some of the surrounding territory. However
such bombs might very well prove to be too heavy for transportation by
air.
SZILÁRD PRODUCED A VERSION TO BE DELIVERED TO PRESIDENT FRANKLIN ROOSEVELT. HE WENT TO EINSTEIN FOR A SIGNATURE, THIS TIME DRIVEN OUT TO LONG ISLAND BY A THIRD HUNGARIAN PHYSICIST, EDWARD TELLER.

EINSTEIN SIGNED...

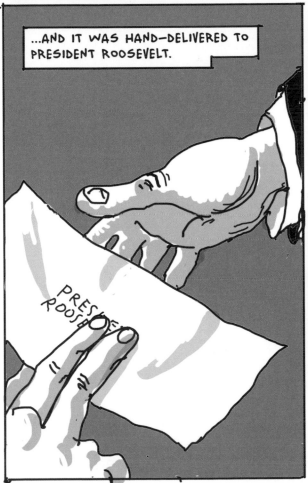

...AND IT WAS HAND-DELIVERED TO PRESIDENT ROOSEVELT.

PRESIDENT ROOSE

THE LETTER IS SEEN BY MANY AS THE START OF THE U.S. EFFORT TO BUILD AN ATOMIC BOMB, CULMINATING SIX YEARS LATER IN THE BOMBING OF JAPAN AND THE SUBSEQUENT DEATH OF AS MANY AS 200,000 CITIZENS IN THE CITIES OF HIROSHIMA AND NAGASAKI.

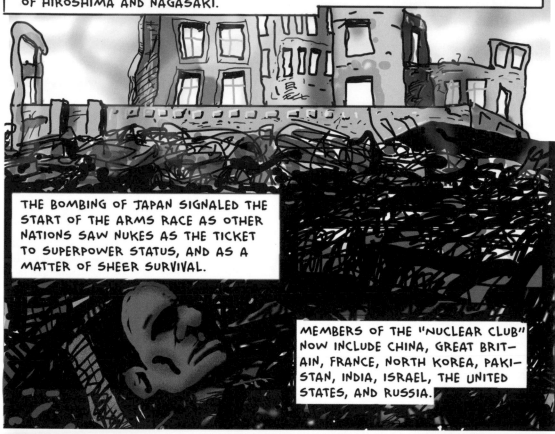

THE BOMBING OF JAPAN SIGNALED THE START OF THE ARMS RACE AS OTHER NATIONS SAW NUKES AS THE TICKET TO SUPERPOWER STATUS, AND AS A MATTER OF SHEER SURVIVAL.

MEMBERS OF THE "NUCLEAR CLUB" NOW INCLUDE CHINA, GREAT BRITAIN, FRANCE, NORTH KOREA, PAKISTAN, INDIA, ISRAEL, THE UNITED STATES, AND RUSSIA.

THE TESTING OF ATOMIC WEAPONS ABOVEGROUND LED TO RADIOACTIVE POLLUTION ON A WORLDWIDE SCALE.

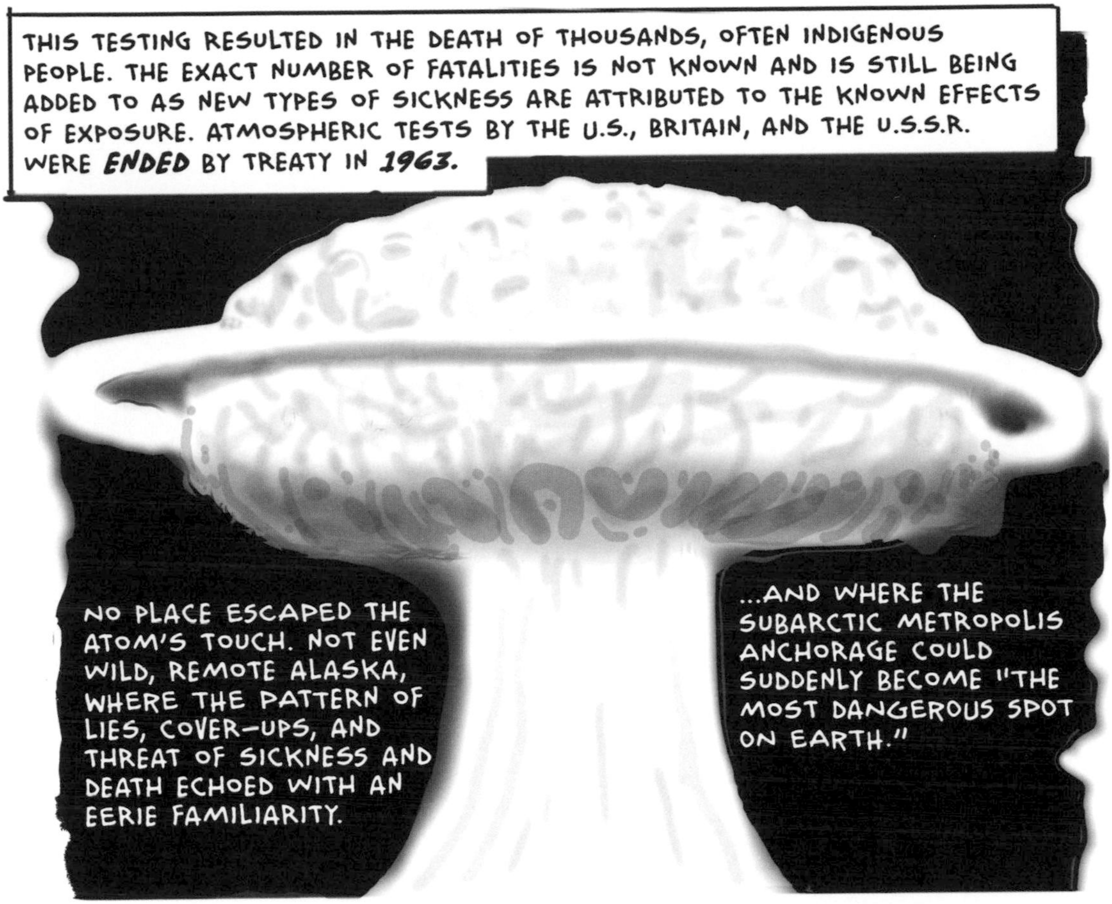
THIS TESTING RESULTED IN THE DEATH OF THOUSANDS, OFTEN INDIGENOUS PEOPLE. THE EXACT NUMBER OF FATALITIES IS NOT KNOWN AND IS STILL BEING ADDED TO AS NEW TYPES OF SICKNESS ARE ATTRIBUTED TO THE KNOWN EFFECTS OF EXPOSURE. ATMOSPHERIC TESTS BY THE U.S., BRITAIN, AND THE U.S.S.R. WERE ENDED BY TREATY IN 1963.
NO PLACE ESCAPED THE ATOM'S TOUCH. NOT EVEN WILD, REMOTE ALASKA, WHERE THE PATTERN OF LIES, COVER-UPS, AND THREAT OF SICKNESS AND DEATH ECHOED WITH AN EERIE FAMILIARITY.
...AND WHERE THE SUBARCTIC METROPOLIS ANCHORAGE COULD SUDDENLY BECOME "THE MOST DANGEROUS SPOT ON EARTH."

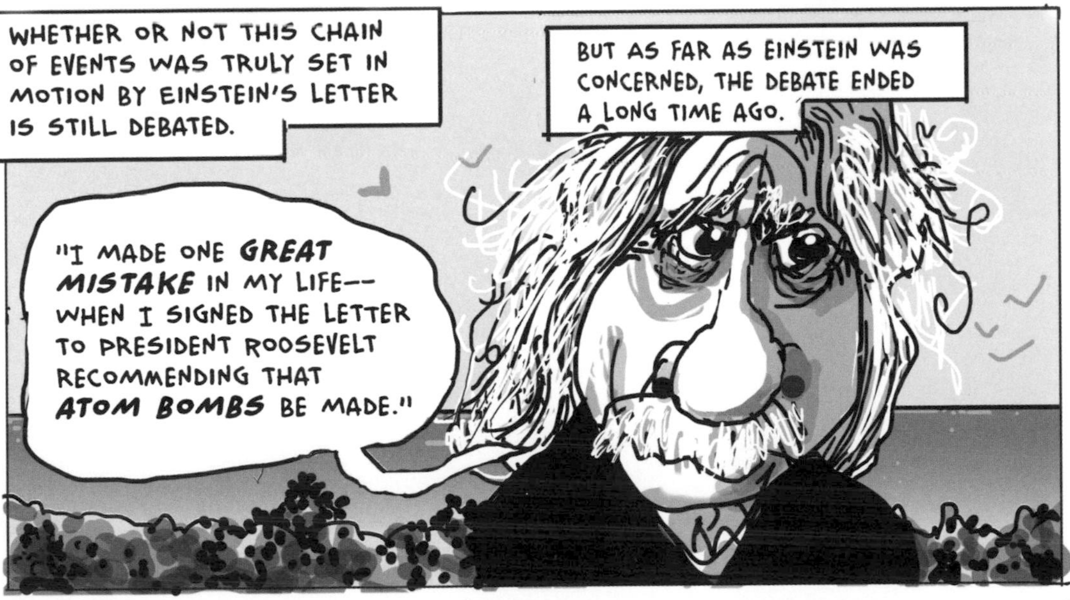
WHETHER OR NOT THIS CHAIN OF EVENTS WAS TRULY SET IN MOTION BY EINSTEIN'S LETTER IS STILL DEBATED.
BUT AS FAR AS EINSTEIN WAS CONCERNED, THE DEBATE ENDED A LONG TIME AGO.
"I MADE ONE GREAT MISTAKE IN MY LIFE-- WHEN I SIGNED THE LETTER TO PRESIDENT ROOSEVELT RECOMMENDING THAT ATOM BOMBS BE MADE."

NUKING ALASKA

1. LABORS OF HERCULES

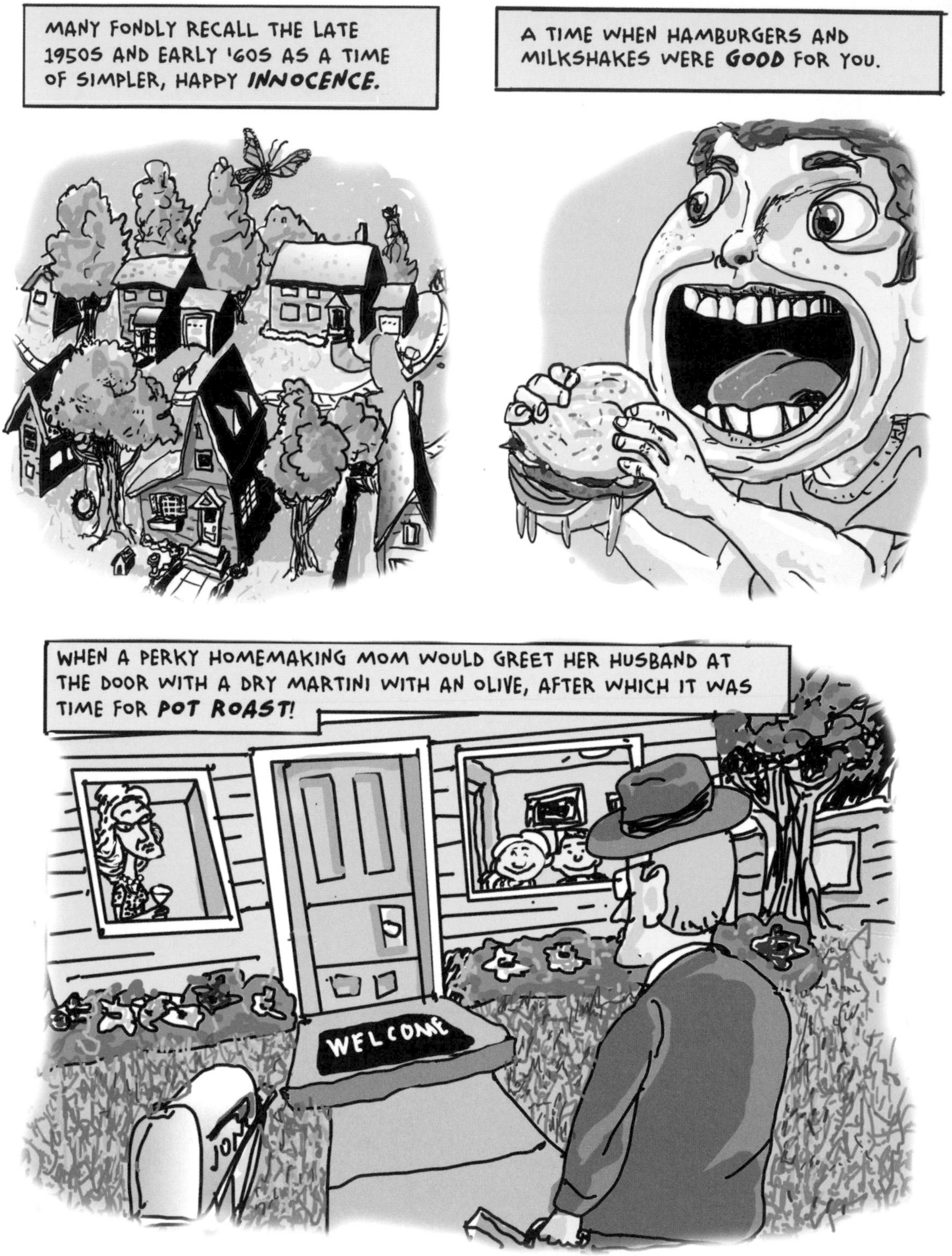
MANY FONDLY RECALL THE LATE 1950S AND EARLY '60S AS A TIME OF SIMPLER, HAPPY INNOCENCE.
A TIME WHEN HAMBURGERS AND MILKSHAKES WERE GOOD FOR YOU.
WHEN A PERKY HOMEMAKING MOM WOULD GREET HER HUSBAND AT THE DOOR WITH A DRY MARTINI WITH AN OLIVE, AFTER WHICH IT WAS TIME FOR POT ROAST!
WELCOME

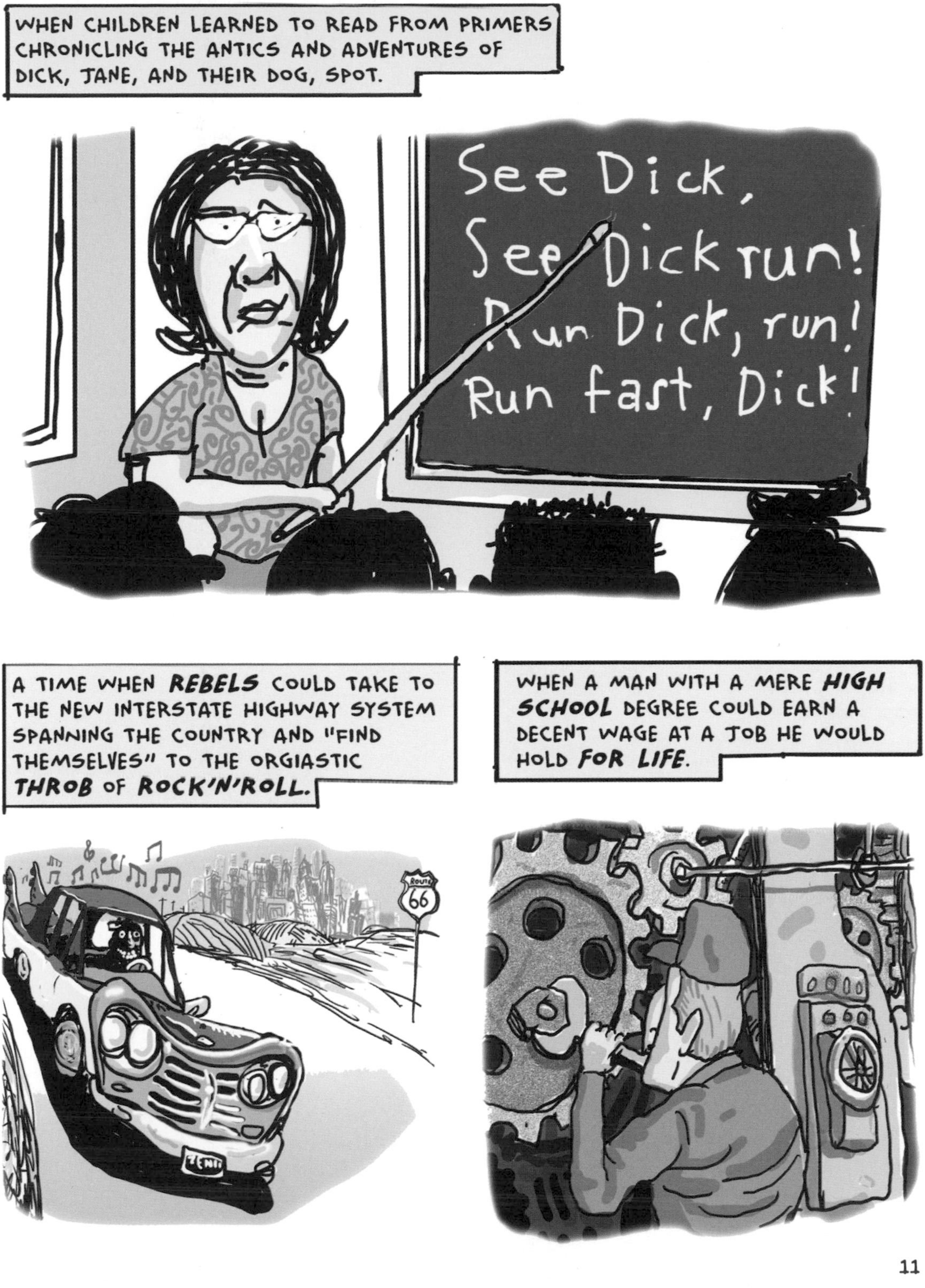
WHEN CHILDREN LEARNED TO READ FROM PRIMERS CHRONICLING THE ANTICS AND ADVENTURES OF DICK, JANE, AND THEIR DOG, SPOT.
See Dick,
See Dick run!
Run Dick, run!
Run fast, Dick!
A TIME WHEN **REBELS** COULD TAKE TO THE NEW INTERSTATE HIGHWAY SYSTEM SPANNING THE COUNTRY AND "FIND THEMSELVES" TO THE ORGIASTIC **THROB** OF **ROCK'N'ROLL.**
ROUTE 66
WHEN A MAN WITH A MERE ***HIGH SCHOOL*** DEGREE COULD EARN A DECENT WAGE AT A JOB HE WOULD HOLD ***FOR LIFE***.

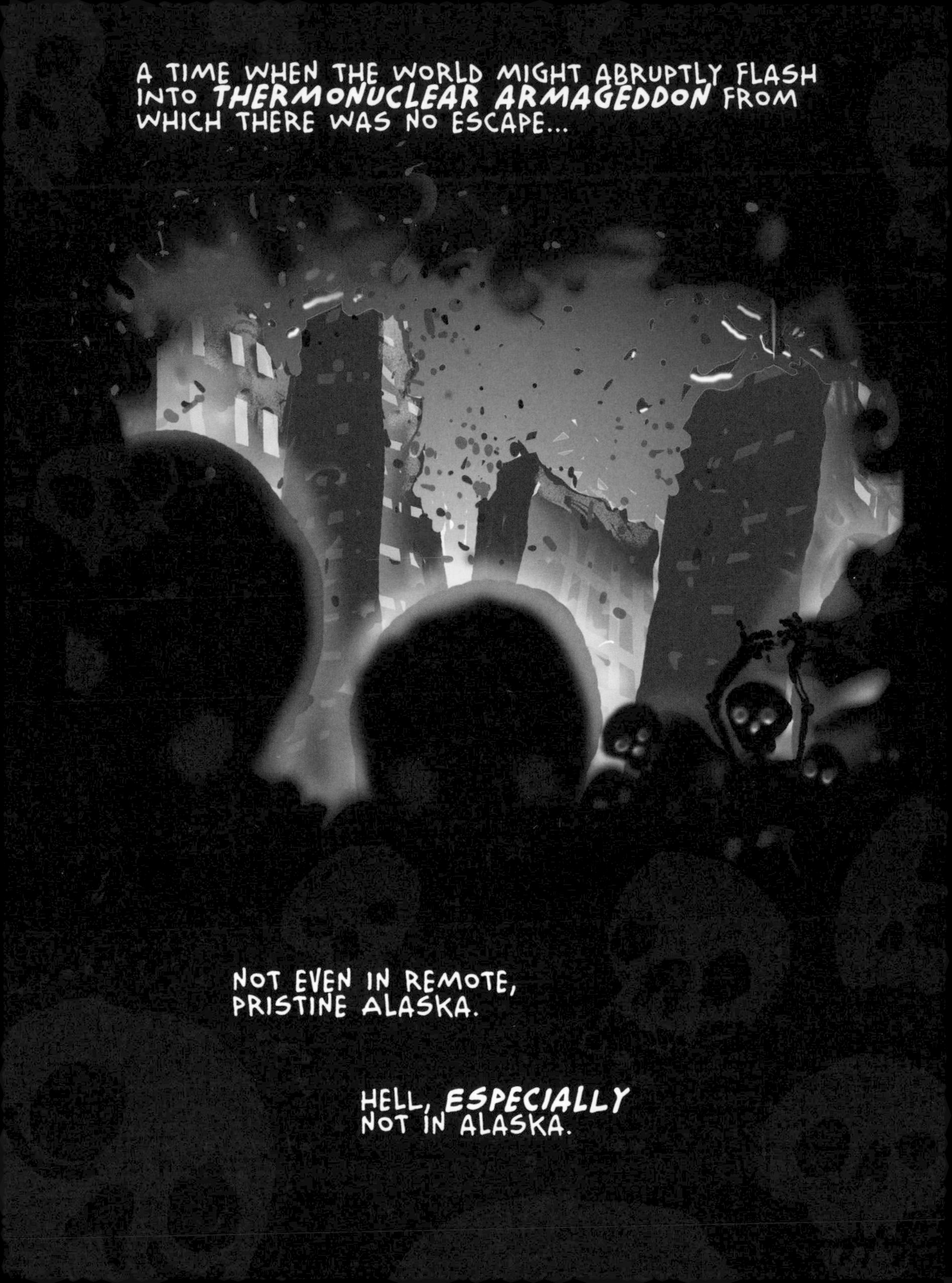
A TIME WHEN THE WORLD MIGHT ABRUPTLY FLASH INTO THERMONUCLEAR ARMAGEDDON FROM WHICH THERE WAS NO ESCAPE...
NOT EVEN IN REMOTE, PRISTINE ALASKA.
HELL, ESPECIALLY NOT IN ALASKA.

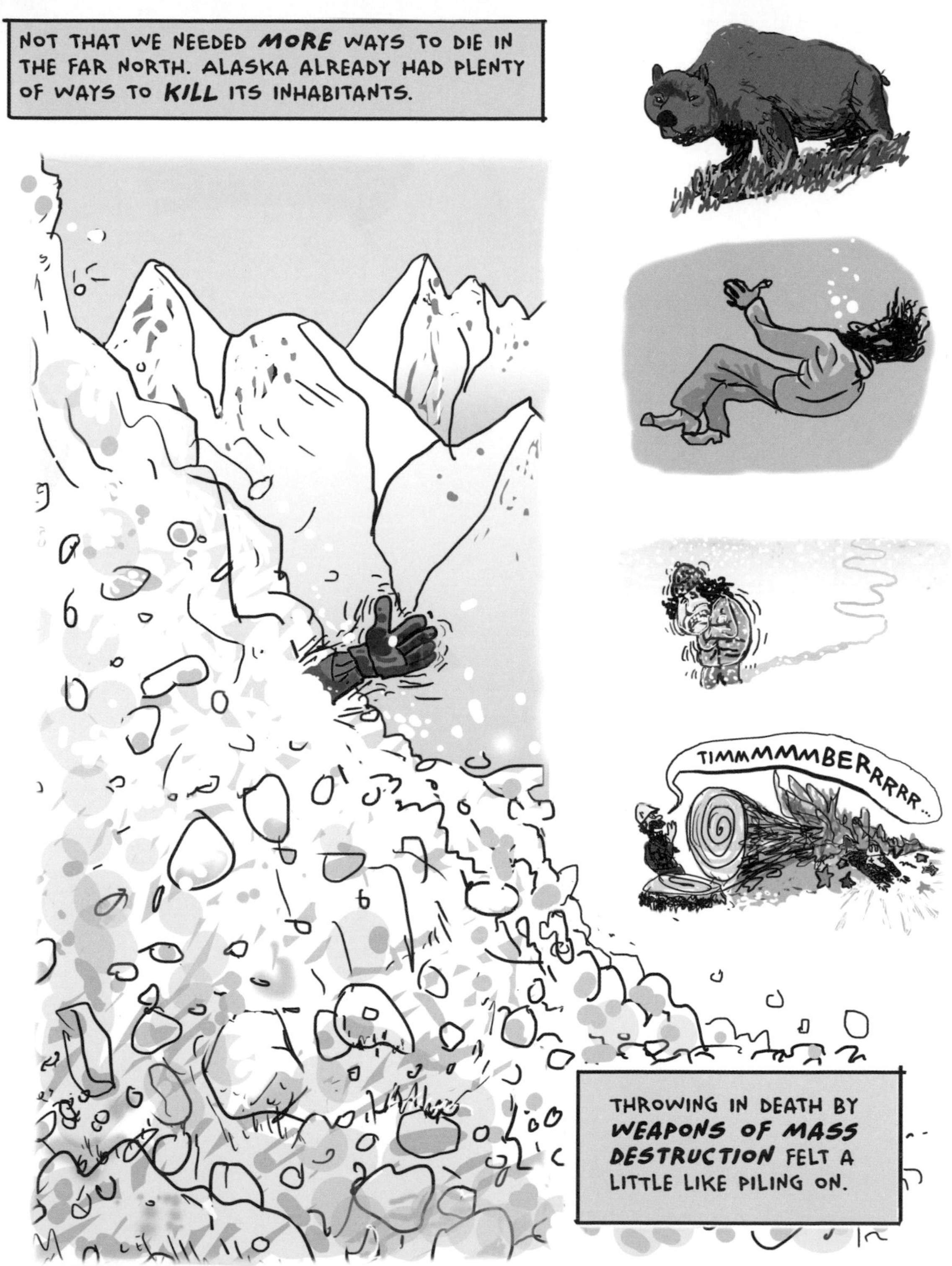
NOT THAT WE NEEDED MORE WAYS TO DIE IN THE FAR NORTH. ALASKA ALREADY HAD PLENTY OF WAYS TO KILL ITS INHABITANTS.
TIMMMMMMBERRRRR...
THROWING IN DEATH BY WEAPONS OF MASS DESTRUCTION FELT A LITTLE LIKE PILING ON.

LIKE MANY MISGUIDED PLANS, THE IDEA OF NUKING ALASKA GOT ITS START IN THE FORMER SOVIET UNION.

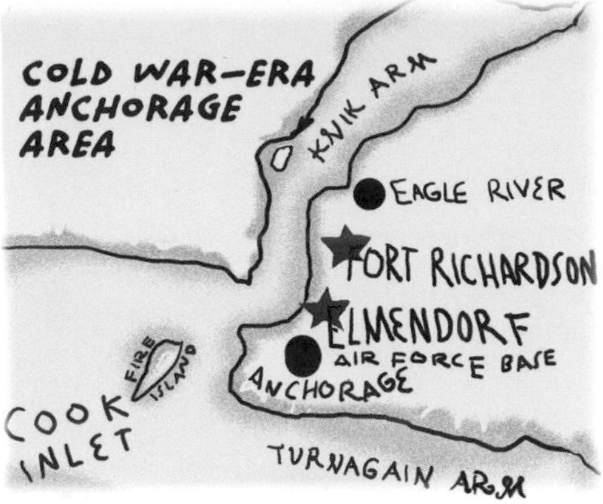
COLD WAR-ERA ANCHORAGE AREA
KNIK ARM
EAGLE RIVER
FORT RICHARDSON
ELMENDORF AIR FORCE BASE
ANCHORAGE
FIRE ISLAND
COOK INLET
TURNAGAIN ARM

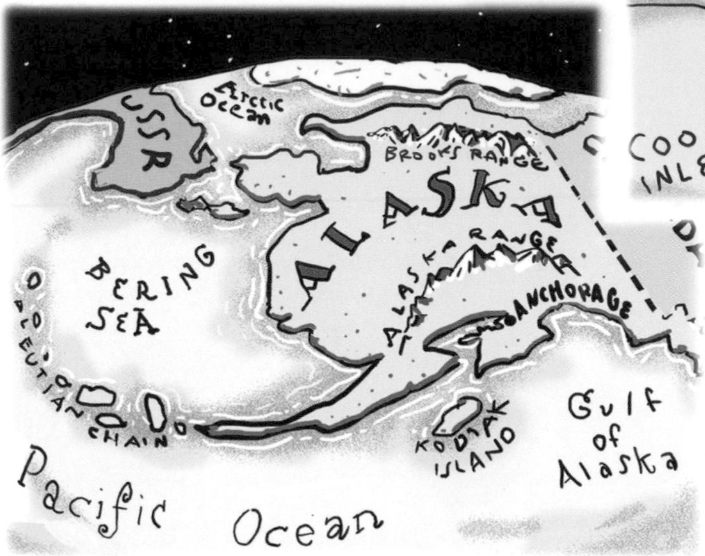
USSR
Arctic Ocean
BROOKS RANGE
ALASKA
ALASKA RANGE
ANCHORAGE
BERING SEA
ALEUTIAN CHAIN
KODIAK ISLAND
Gulf of Alaska
Pacific Ocean

IT WASN'T ANYTHING PERSONAL. **GEOGRAPHY** PUT ALASKA ON THE FRONT LINES OF THE COLD WAR.

A CHAIN OF RADARS, THE DISTANT EARLY WARNING SYSTEM, OR DEW LINE, PROBED THE SKY ABOVE OUR BORDER FOR POSSIBLE AIRBORNE ATTACKS.

BOTH SIDES KEPT NUCLEAR-ARMED BOMBERS ON CONSTANT PATROLS AS WELL AS MISSILE-ARMED SUBS UNDER THE SEAS AND LAND-BASED MISSILES READY TO LAUNCH FROM THEIR SILOS.

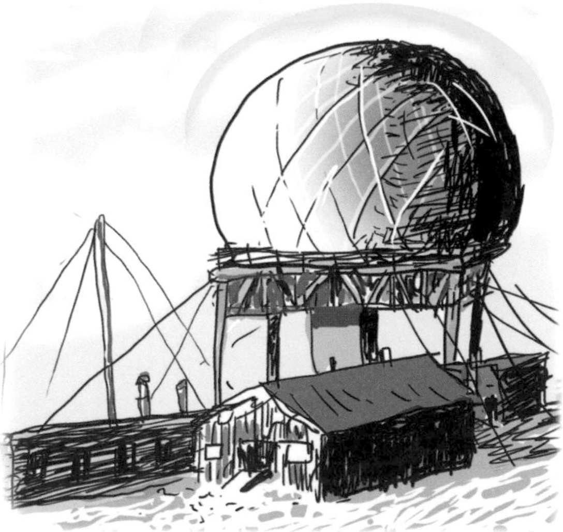

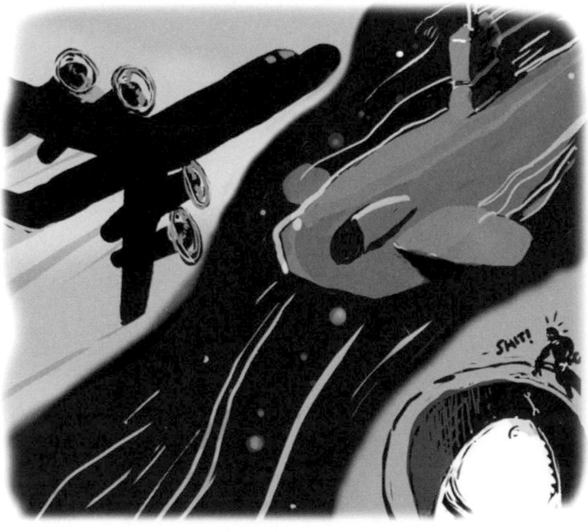
SHIT!

FEAR FESTERED AS THE SOVIETS MADE THE FIRST LEAP INTO OUTER SPACE, WITH THE LAUNCH OF A SATELLITE NAMED SPUTNIK IN 1958.

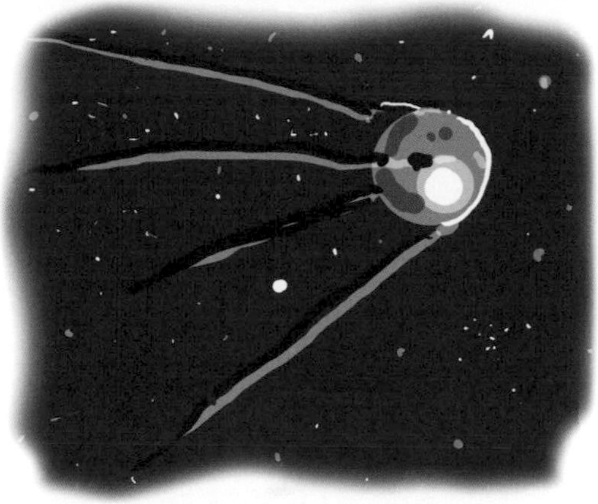

DURING THE 1960 PRESIDENTIAL RACE, JOHN F. KENNEDY AGGRAVATED THE NUCLEAR WORRIES OF THE FRIGHTENED NATION.

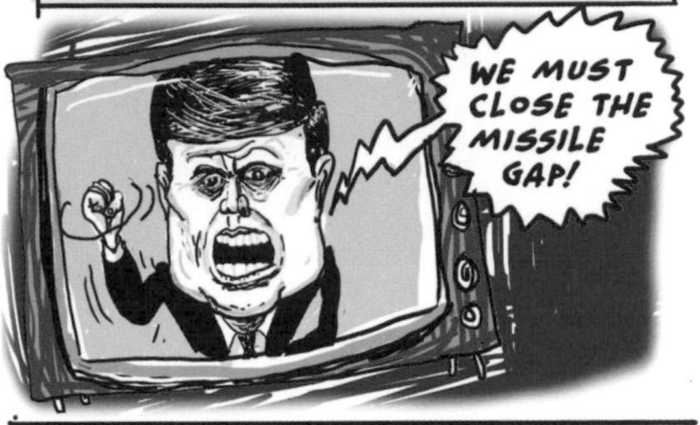
WE MUST CLOSE THE MISSILE GAP!

IN FACT, THE U.S. HAD ***NINE*** TIMES THE NUMBER OF NUCLEAR WEAPONS THAN WERE IN THE SOVIET ARSENAL.

SOVIET PREMIER NIKITA KHRUSHCHEV WAS NOT A REASSURING PRESENCE. HIS FAMOUS ***OUTBURST*** AT THE POLISH EMBASSY IS ONE EXAMPLE.

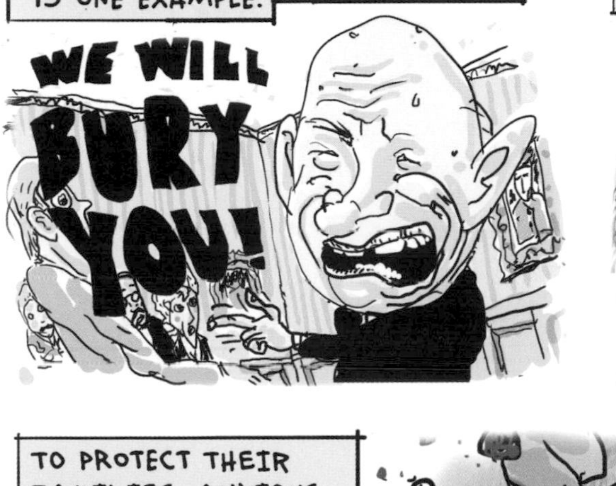
WE WILL BURY YOU!

THEN, ***PROVOKED*** BY THE BAY OF PIGS INVASION OF CUBA AND U.S. DEPLOYMENT OF MISSILES IN TURKEY, THE SOVIETS TRIED TO SNEAK MISSILES INTO CUBA.

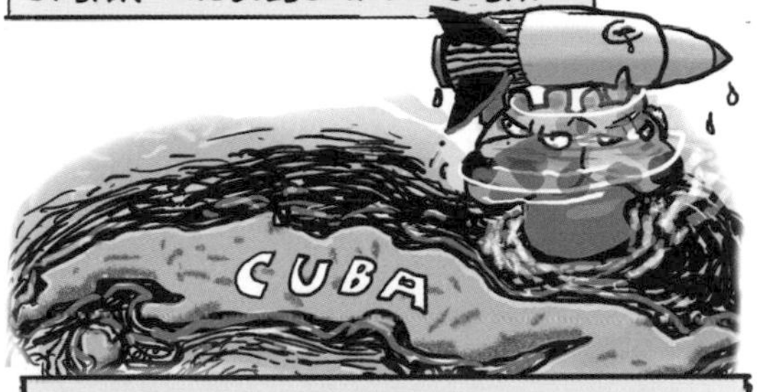
CUBA

THE ***"CUBAN MISSILE CRISIS"*** ENSUED, SCARING THE ***CRAP*** OUT OF EVERYONE.

TO PROTECT THEIR FAMILIES, ANXIOUS CITIZENS DUG ***FALLOUT*** SHELTERS IN THEIR ***BACKYARDS.***

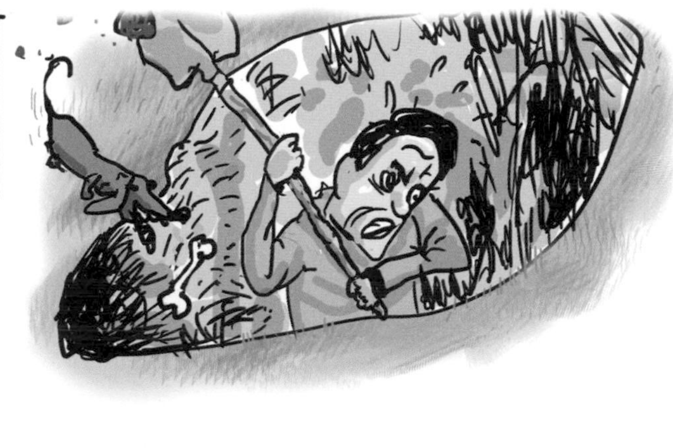

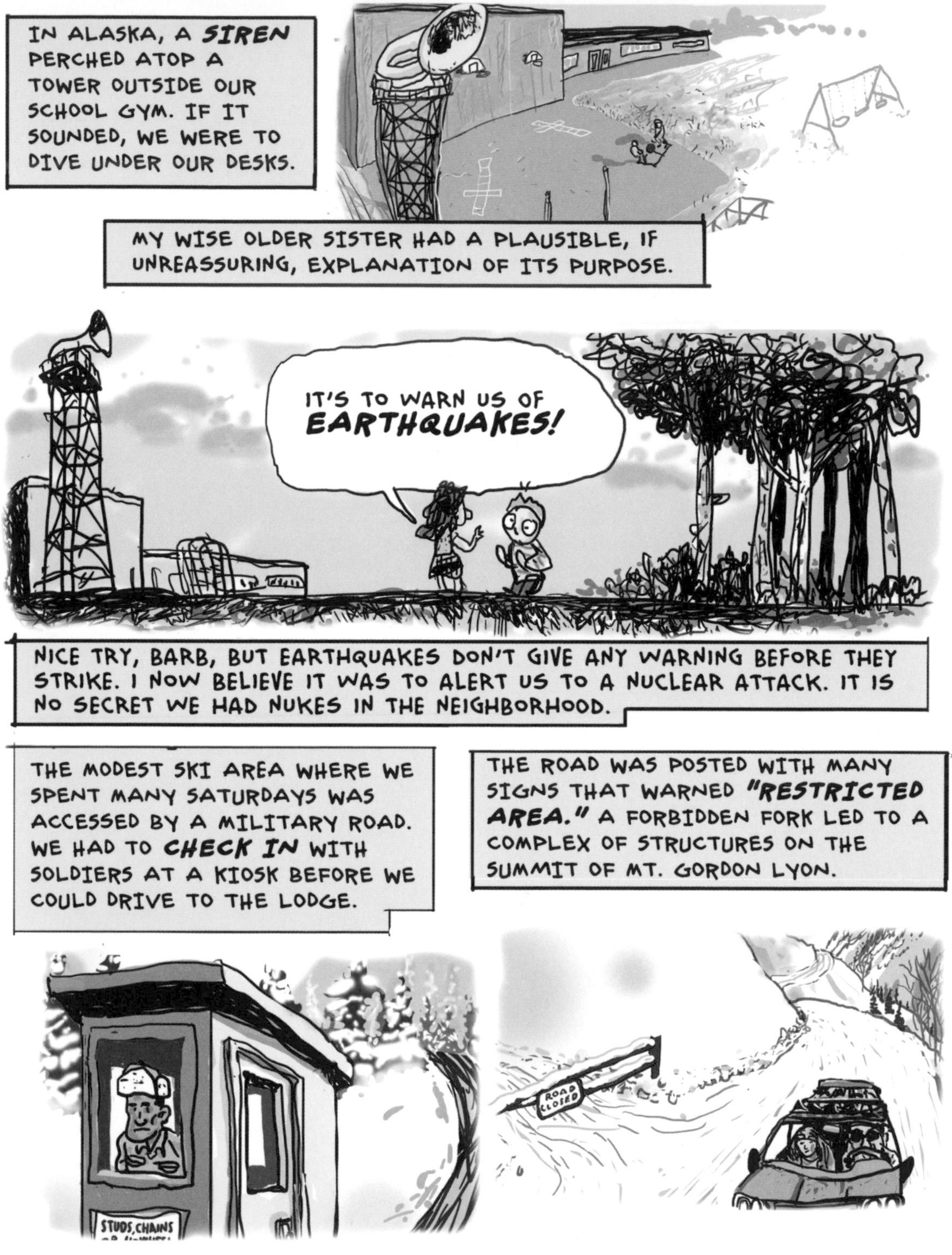

IN ALASKA, A SIREN PERCHED ATOP A TOWER OUTSIDE OUR SCHOOL GYM. IF IT SOUNDED, WE WERE TO DIVE UNDER OUR DESKS.
MY WISE OLDER SISTER HAD A PLAUSIBLE, IF UNREASSURING, EXPLANATION OF ITS PURPOSE.
IT'S TO WARN US OF EARTHQUAKES!
NICE TRY, BARB, BUT EARTHQUAKES DON'T GIVE ANY WARNING BEFORE THEY STRIKE. I NOW BELIEVE IT WAS TO ALERT US TO A NUCLEAR ATTACK. IT IS NO SECRET WE HAD NUKES IN THE NEIGHBORHOOD.
THE MODEST SKI AREA WHERE WE SPENT MANY SATURDAYS WAS ACCESSED BY A MILITARY ROAD. WE HAD TO CHECK IN WITH SOLDIERS AT A KIOSK BEFORE WE COULD DRIVE TO THE LODGE.
THE ROAD WAS POSTED WITH MANY SIGNS THAT WARNED "RESTRICTED AREA." A FORBIDDEN FORK LED TO A COMPLEX OF STRUCTURES ON THE SUMMIT OF MT. GORDON LYON.
STUDS,CHAINS
ROAD CLOSED

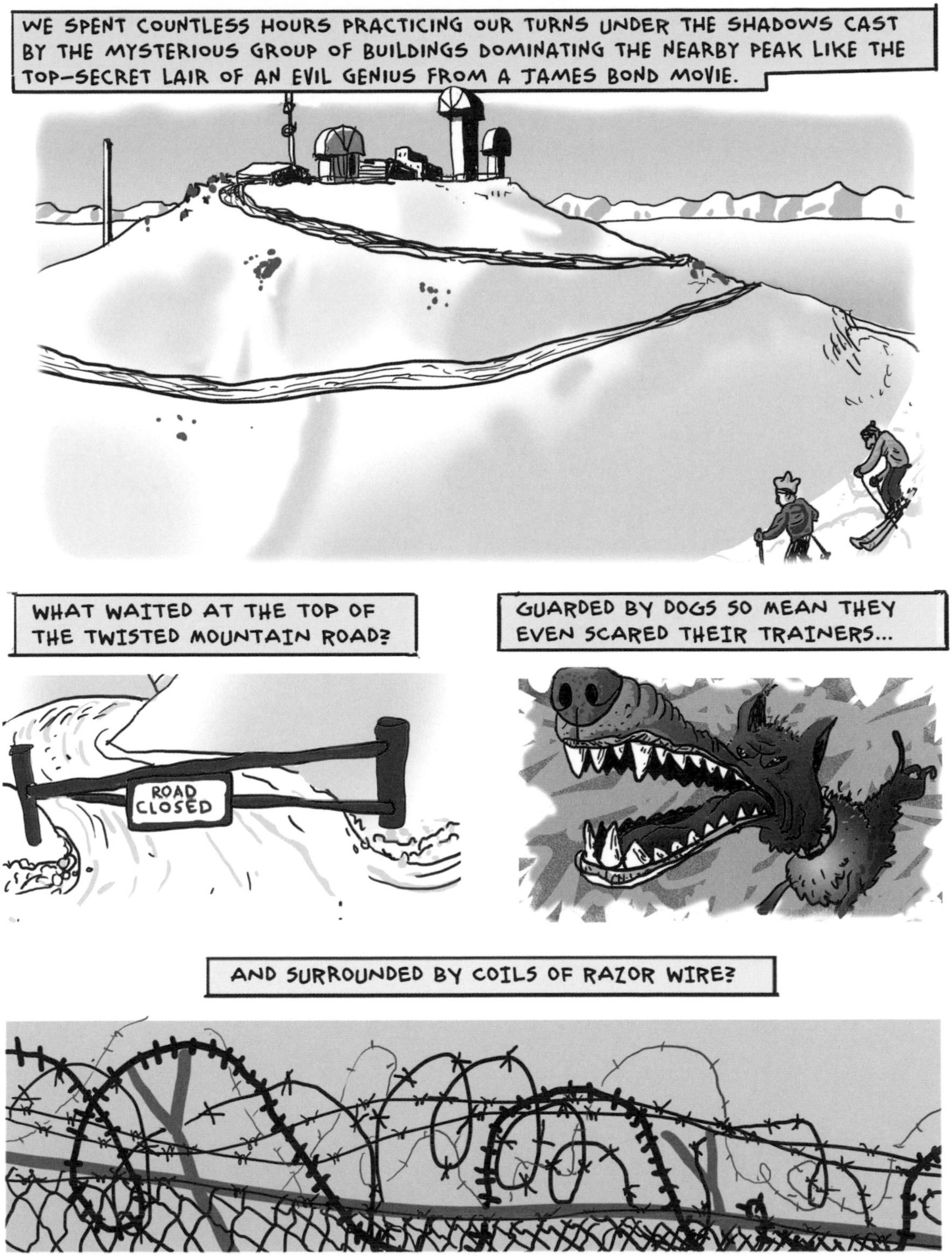
WE SPENT COUNTLESS HOURS PRACTICING OUR TURNS UNDER THE SHADOWS CAST BY THE MYSTERIOUS GROUP OF BUILDINGS DOMINATING THE NEARBY PEAK LIKE THE TOP-SECRET LAIR OF AN EVIL GENIUS FROM A JAMES BOND MOVIE.
WHAT WAITED AT THE TOP OF THE TWISTED MOUNTAIN ROAD?
ROAD CLOSED
GUARDED BY DOGS SO MEAN THEY EVEN SCARED THEIR TRAINERS...
AND SURROUNDED BY COILS OF RAZOR WIRE?

IT WAS THE ***SWORD OF DAMOCLES*** IN THE FORM OF A NIKE HERCULES NUCLEAR-ARMED MISSILE (BUT YOU MAY CALL IT BY ITS FRIENDLY NICKNAME, ***SAM,*** SHORT FOR SURFACE-TO-AIR MISSILE).

THE NIKE HERCULES MISSILE

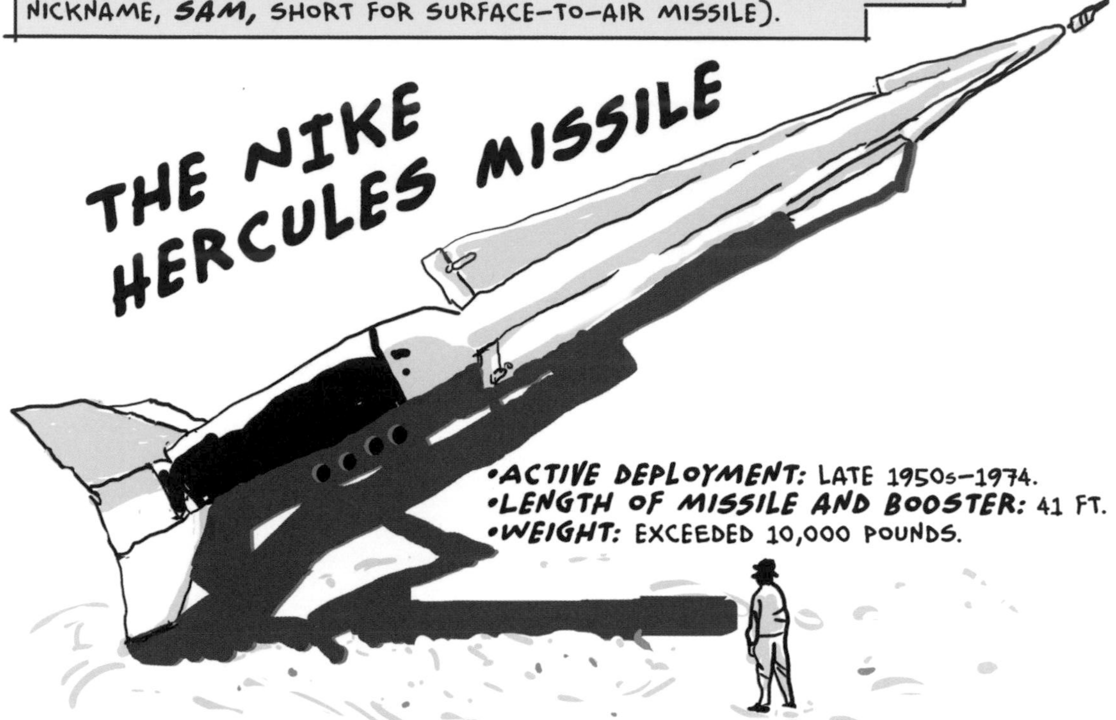

- ***ACTIVE DEPLOYMENT:*** LATE 1950s–1974.
- ***LENGTH OF MISSILE AND BOOSTER:*** 41 FT.
- ***WEIGHT:*** EXCEEDED 10,000 POUNDS.

- TOP SPEED WAS 2,707. MILES PER HOUR.
- THE HERCULES HAD A RANGE OF 80 MILES.
- ABLE TO REACH TARGETS AT ALTITUDES OF UP TO 100,000 FT.
- BURNED SOLID FUEL.
- AT U.S. SITES, ALMOST EXCLUSIVELY CARRIED A NUCLEAR WARHEAD. THE W-31 WARHEAD HAD FOUR VARIANTS. THE 20-KILOTON VERSION WAS USED IN THE HERCULES SYSTEM.

WORKING AT THE SITE MUST HAVE BEEN LONELY, AND BRUTALLY COLD. THE MAIN BUILDING SHELTERING THE SOLDIERS HAD TO BE ANCHORED TO THE GROUND TO SURVIVE THE RELENTLESS WINDS.

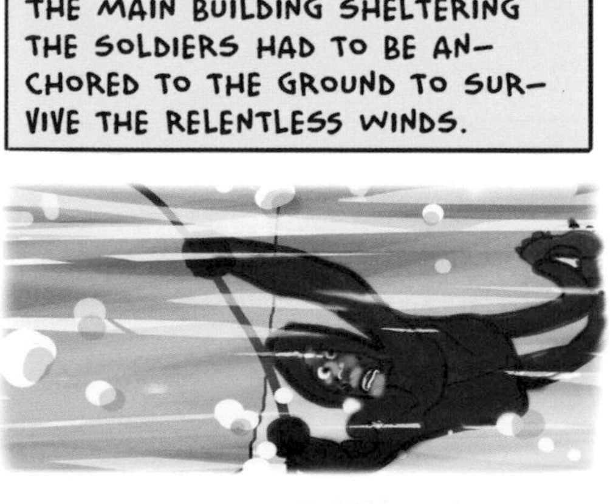

THE AREA WAS PATROLLED 24 HOURS A DAY, SEVEN DAYS A WEEK BY A GUARD WITH A FIERCE DOG, TRAINED ON-SITE.

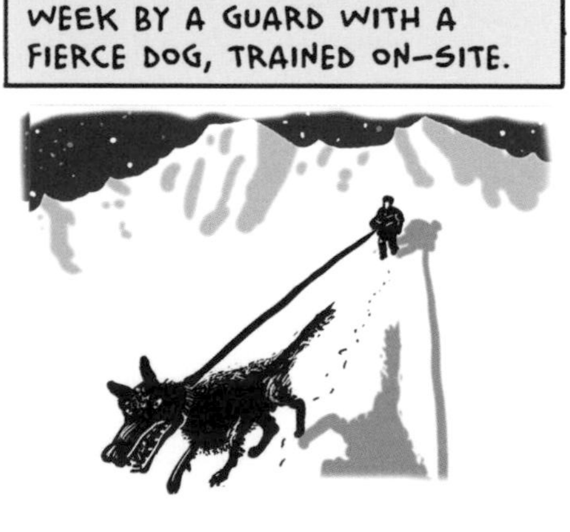

THE MOST INTRIGUING BUILDINGS ON THE SITE, THE RADAR "CLAMSHELLS," DETERIORATED WITH THE PASSAGE OF TIME.

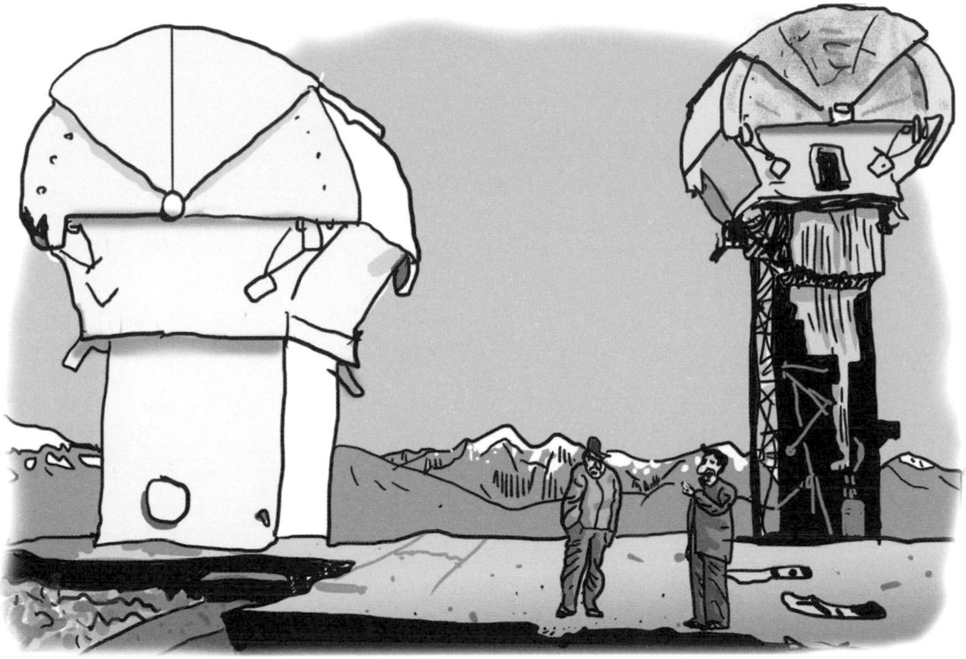

THE FOLDING SHELLS WERE INSPIRED BY JAPANESE ORIGAMI AND UNIQUE TO THE HARSH LOCATION, PROTECTING THE RADAR FROM WINDS THAT COULD REACH 120 KNOTS (ALMOST 140 MPH).

THE MISSILES WERE STORED IN CONCRETE BUNKERS, WITH TRACKS ON WHICH THEY COULD ROLL OUT FOR LAUNCH.

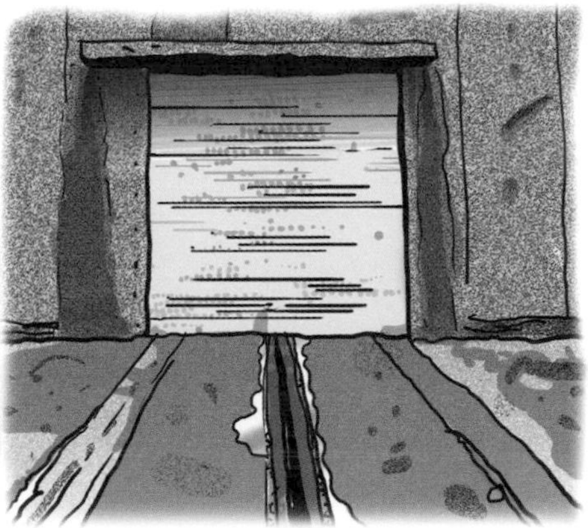

THE PLAN WAS TO GET THEM ALOFT SOON ENOUGH TO KNOCK DOWN INCOMING BOMBERS WITH A 20-KILOTON NUCLEAR WARHEAD.

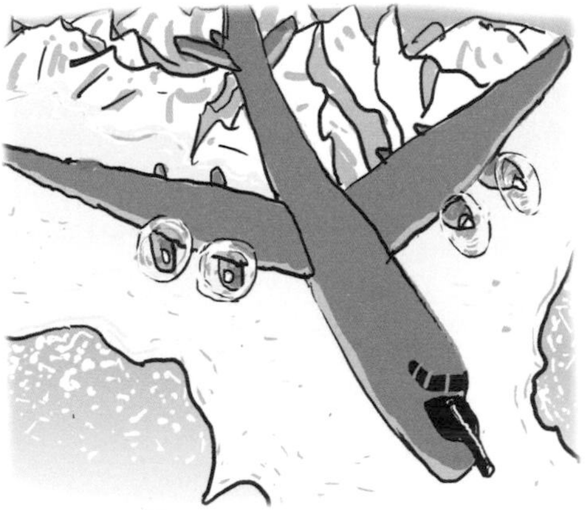

THE MISSILES' 80-MILE RANGE MEANT ANCHORAGE'S BEST HOPE IN CASE OF ***ARMAGEDDON*** WAS A STRIKE OVER THE HAMLET OF WILLOW--AND A STRONG BREEZE OUT OF THE SOUTH.

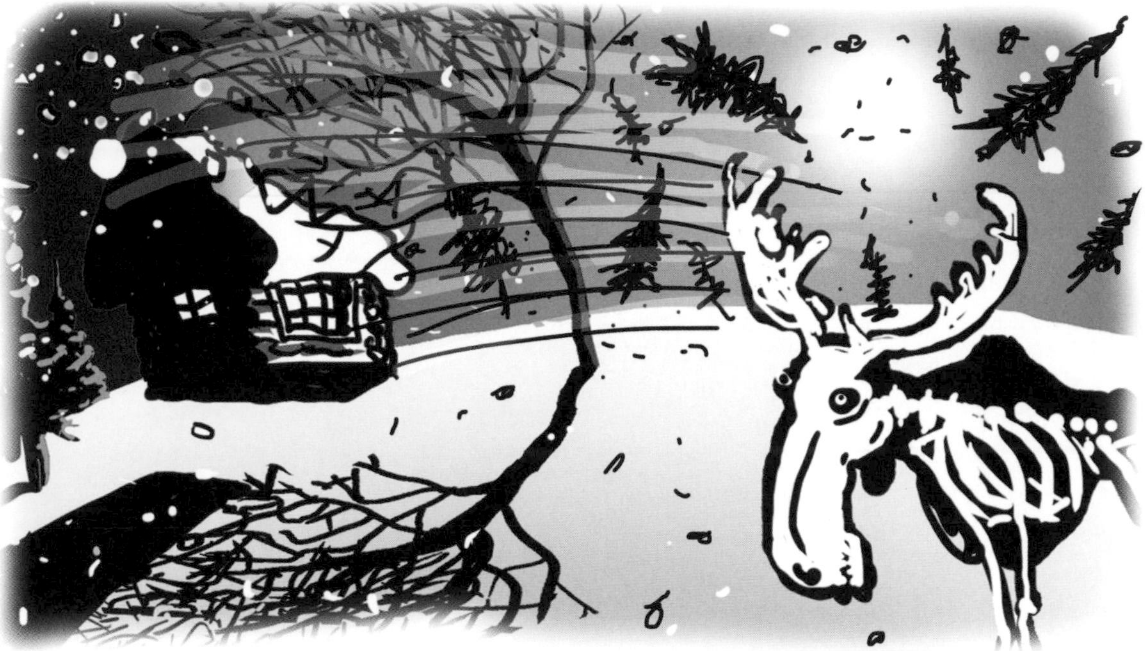

SOMEWHERE IN THE BACK OF OUR MINDS, WE WERE ALWAYS WAITING FOR THE SOUND OF THOSE BOMBERS.

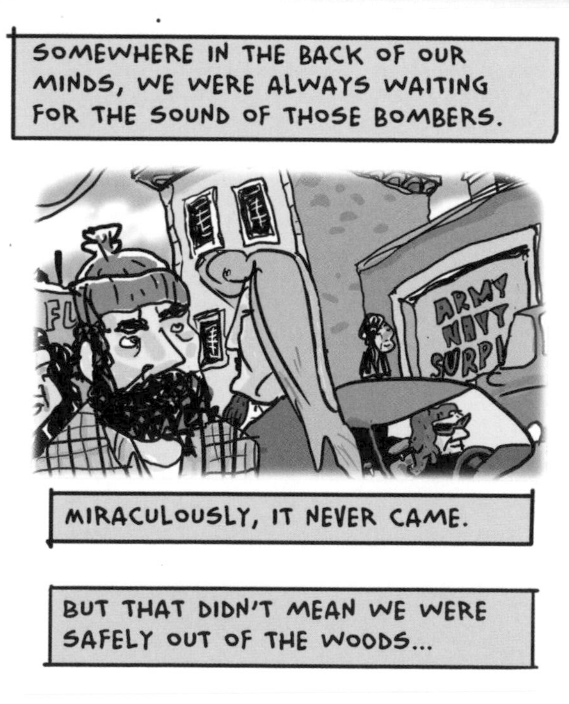
ARMY
NAVY
SURP

MIRACULOUSLY, IT NEVER CAME.

BUT THAT DIDN'T MEAN WE WERE SAFELY OUT OF THE WOODS...

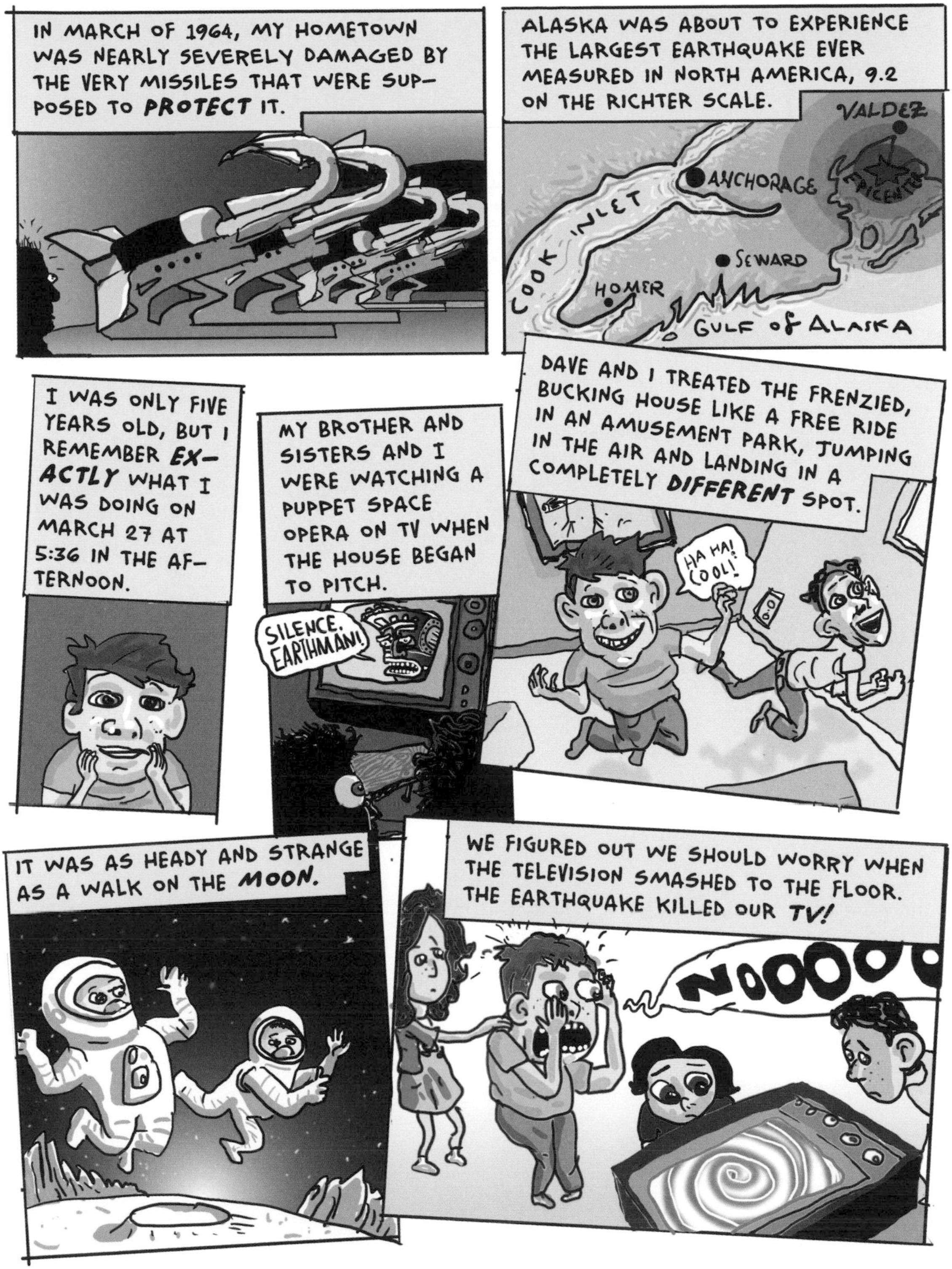
IN MARCH OF 1964, MY HOMETOWN WAS NEARLY SEVERELY DAMAGED BY THE VERY MISSILES THAT WERE SUPPOSED TO PROTECT IT.
ALASKA WAS ABOUT TO EXPERIENCE THE LARGEST EARTHQUAKE EVER MEASURED IN NORTH AMERICA, 9.2 ON THE RICHTER SCALE.
VALDEZ
ANCHORAGE
EPICENTER
COOK INLET
SEWARD
HOMER
GULF OF ALASKA
I WAS ONLY FIVE YEARS OLD, BUT I REMEMBER EXACTLY WHAT I WAS DOING ON MARCH 27 AT 5:36 IN THE AFTERNOON.
MY BROTHER AND SISTERS AND I WERE WATCHING A PUPPET SPACE OPERA ON TV WHEN THE HOUSE BEGAN TO PITCH.
SILENCE. EARTHMAN!
DAVE AND I TREATED THE FRENZIED, BUCKING HOUSE LIKE A FREE RIDE IN AN AMUSEMENT PARK, JUMPING IN THE AIR AND LANDING IN A COMPLETELY DIFFERENT SPOT.
HA HA! COOL!
IT WAS AS HEADY AND STRANGE AS A WALK ON THE MOON.
WE FIGURED OUT WE SHOULD WORRY WHEN THE TELEVISION SMASHED TO THE FLOOR. THE EARTHQUAKE KILLED OUR TV!
NOOOOO

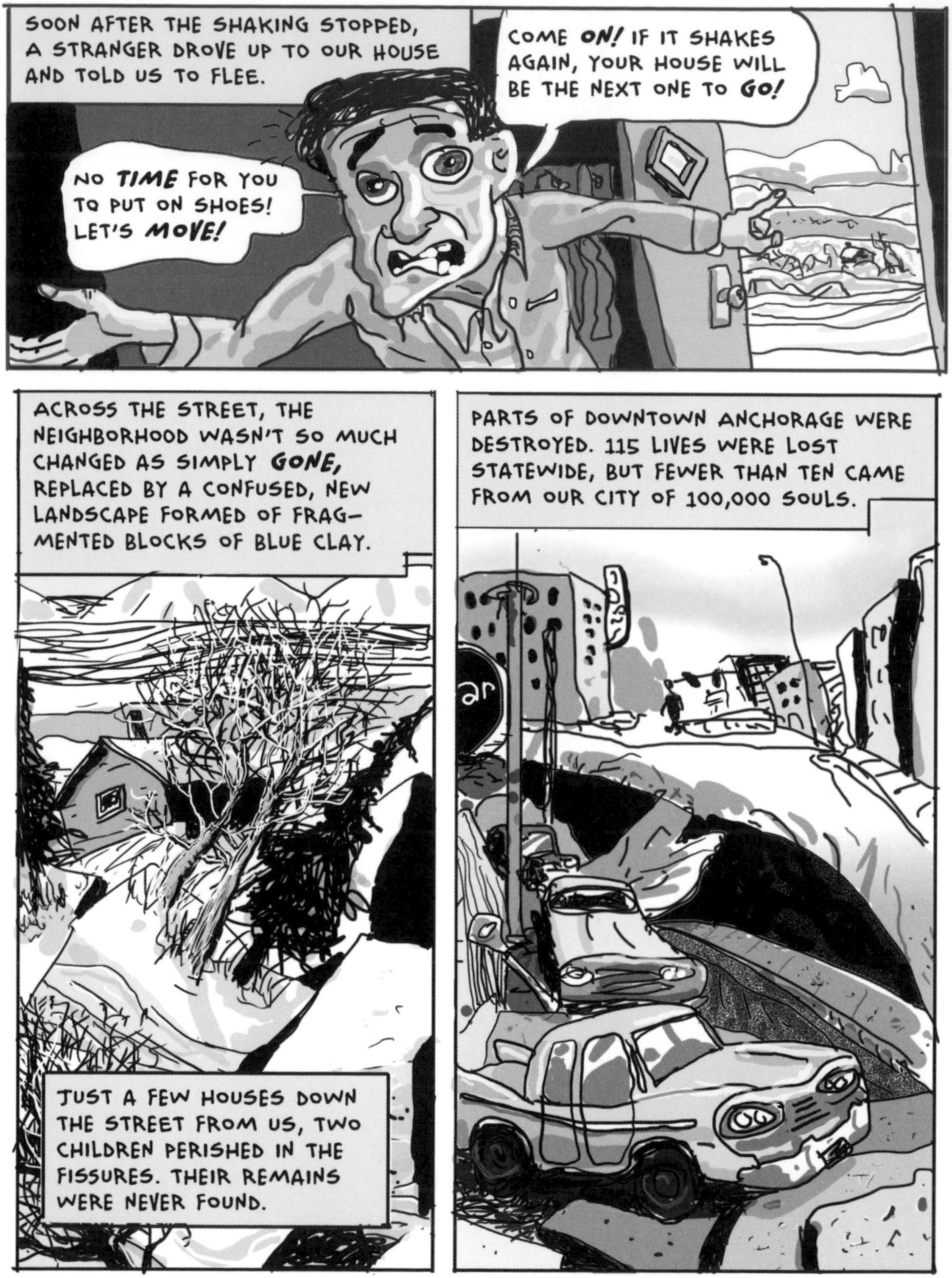
SOON AFTER THE SHAKING STOPPED, A STRANGER DROVE UP TO OUR HOUSE AND TOLD US TO FLEE.
COME ON! IF IT SHAKES AGAIN, YOUR HOUSE WILL BE THE NEXT ONE TO GO!
NO TIME FOR YOU TO PUT ON SHOES! LET'S MOVE!
ACROSS THE STREET, THE NEIGHBORHOOD WASN'T SO MUCH CHANGED AS SIMPLY GONE, REPLACED BY A CONFUSED, NEW LANDSCAPE FORMED OF FRAGMENTED BLOCKS OF BLUE CLAY.
JUST A FEW HOUSES DOWN THE STREET FROM US, TWO CHILDREN PERISHED IN THE FISSURES. THEIR REMAINS WERE NEVER FOUND.
PARTS OF DOWNTOWN ANCHORAGE WERE DESTROYED. 115 LIVES WERE LOST STATEWIDE, BUT FEWER THAN TEN CAME FROM OUR CITY OF 100,000 SOULS.

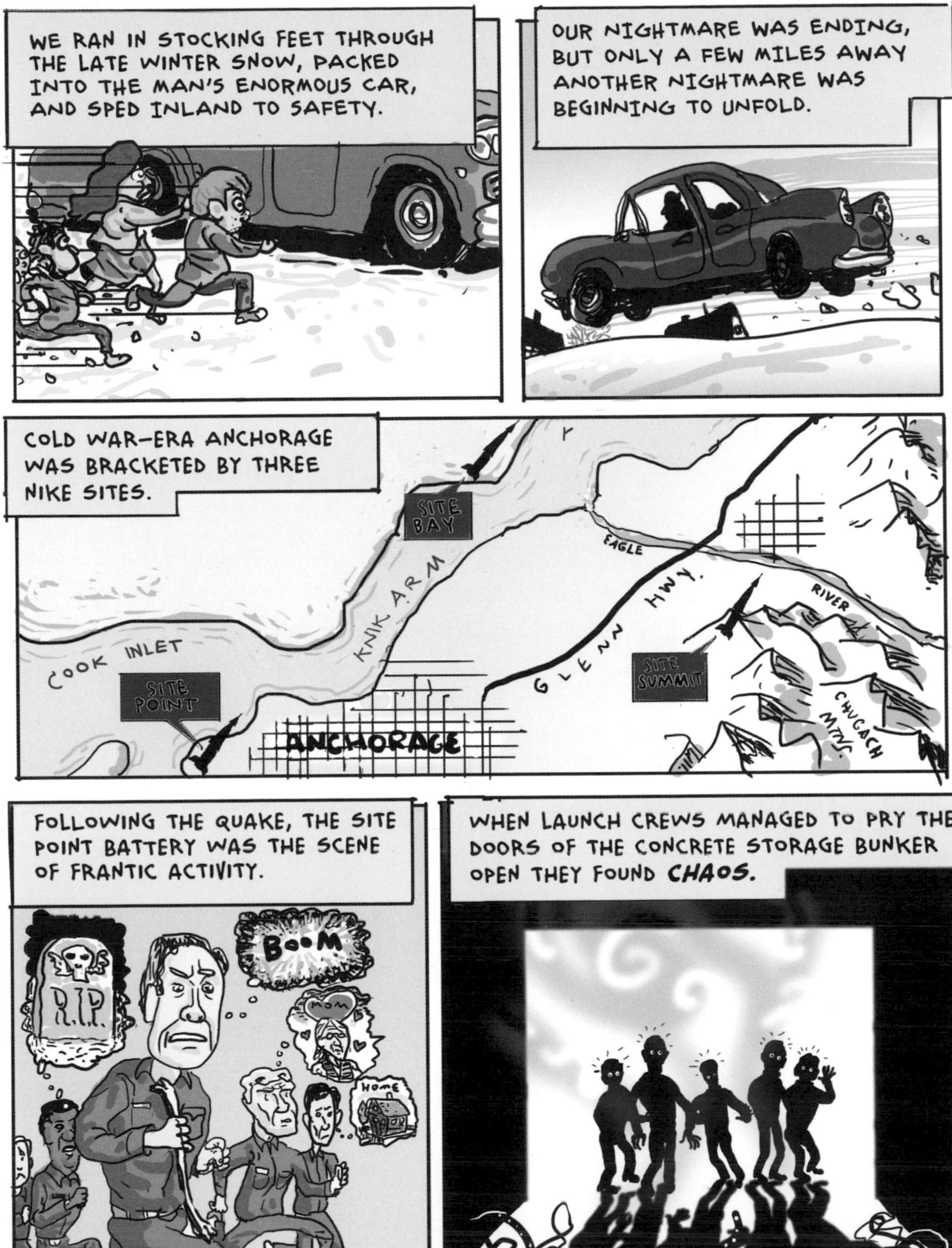
WE RAN IN STOCKING FEET THROUGH THE LATE WINTER SNOW, PACKED INTO THE MAN'S ENORMOUS CAR, AND SPED INLAND TO SAFETY.
OUR NIGHTMARE WAS ENDING, BUT ONLY A FEW MILES AWAY ANOTHER NIGHTMARE WAS BEGINNING TO UNFOLD.
COLD WAR-ERA ANCHORAGE WAS BRACKETED BY THREE NIKE SITES.
SITE BAY
EAGLE
KNIK ARM
GLENN HWY.
RIVER
COOK INLET
SITE POINT
SITE SUMMIT
CHUGACH MTNS.
ANCHORAGE
FOLLOWING THE QUAKE, THE SITE POINT BATTERY WAS THE SCENE OF FRANTIC ACTIVITY.
R.I.P.
BOOM
MOM
HOME
WHEN LAUNCH CREWS MANAGED TO PRY THE DOORS OF THE CONCRETE STORAGE BUNKER OPEN THEY FOUND CHAOS.

ANATOMY OF A NIKE HERCULES MISSILE

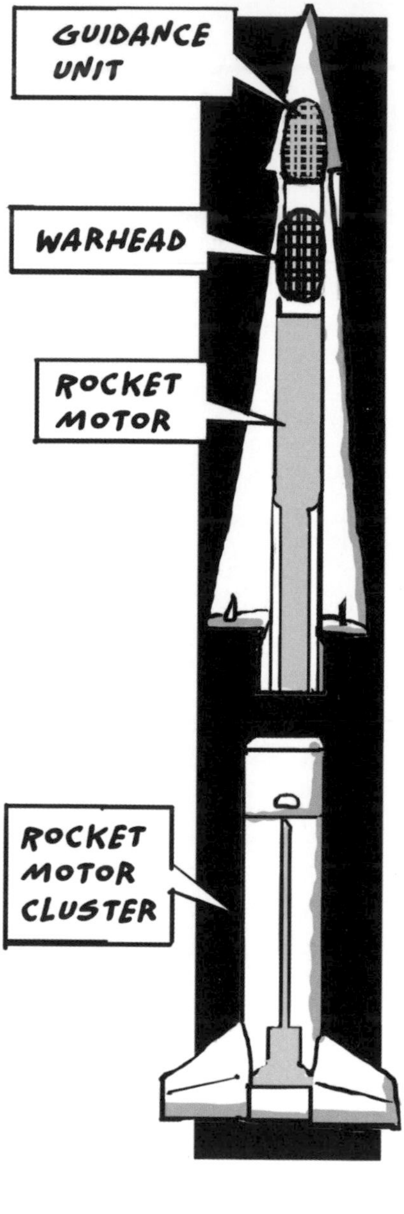
GUIDANCE UNIT
WARHEAD
ROCKET MOTOR
ROCKET MOTOR CLUSTER

THE WARHEAD (SCHEMATIC CROSS SECTION)

THE W31 WARHEAD WAS USED FOR NUCLEAR-EQUIPPED VERSIONS OF THE HERCULES. IT IS A BOOSTED FISSION IMPLOSION DEVICE.

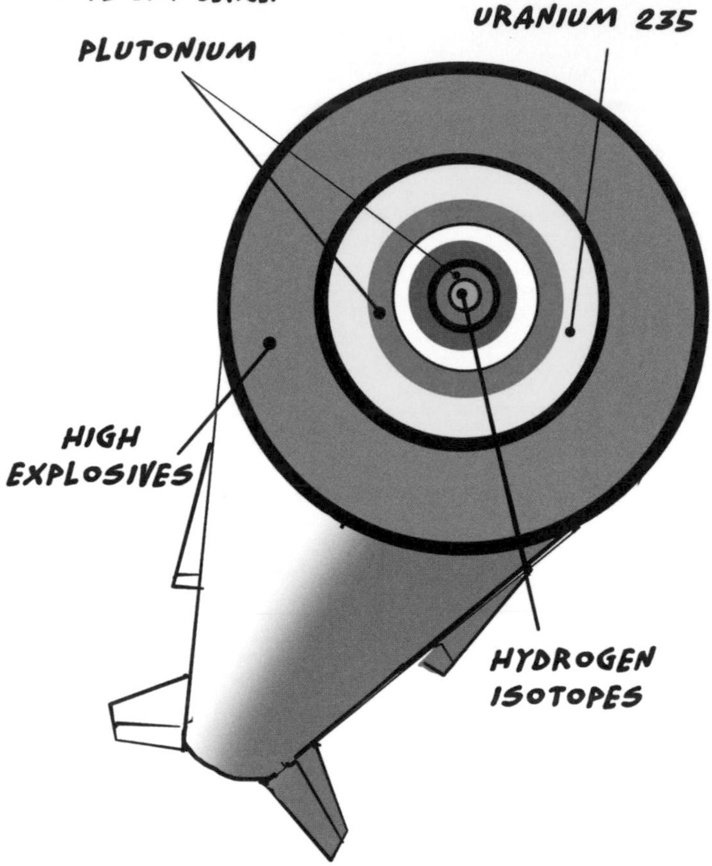
URANIUM 235
PLUTONIUM
HIGH EXPLOSIVES
HYDROGEN ISOTOPES

CREATING A NUCLEAR EXPLOSION IS ***NOT*** EASY. IT REQUIRES TWO MASSES OF FISSILE MATERIAL (PLUTONIUM AND URANIUM 235) THAT ARE CRUSHED TOGETHER, IMPLODED, WITH GREAT FORCE BY THE DETONATION OF CONVENTIONAL EXPLOSIVES. THE SUDDEN COMPRESSION OF THE TWO FISSILE ELEMENTS CREATES A ***CRITICAL MASS,*** STARTING A CHAIN REACTION RELEASING MASSIVE AMOUNTS OF ENERGY. IN BOOSTED FISSION, HYDROGEN MOLECULES ARE PLACED IN THE FISSILE CORE, INCREASING THE PRESSURE AND TEMPERATURE, ACCELERATING FISSION.

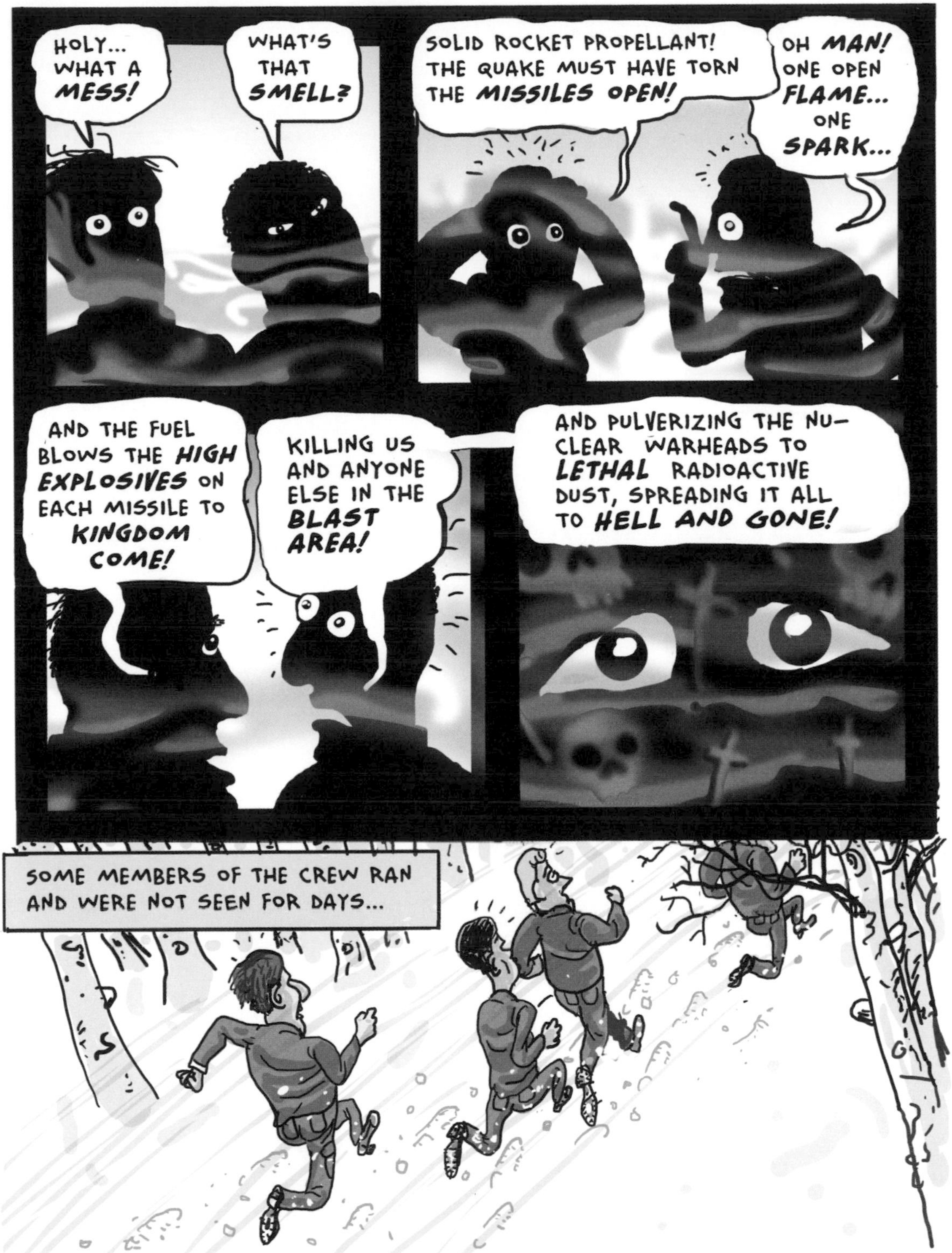
HOLY... WHAT A MESS!
WHAT'S THAT SMELL?
SOLID ROCKET PROPELLANT! THE QUAKE MUST HAVE TORN THE MISSILES OPEN!
OH MAN! ONE OPEN FLAME... ONE SPARK...
AND THE FUEL BLOWS THE HIGH EXPLOSIVES ON EACH MISSILE TO KINGDOM COME!
KILLING US AND ANYONE ELSE IN THE BLAST AREA!
AND PULVERIZING THE NU-CLEAR WARHEADS TO LETHAL RADIOACTIVE DUST, SPREADING IT ALL TO HELL AND GONE!
SOME MEMBERS OF THE CREW RAN AND WERE NOT SEEN FOR DAYS...

GEORGE WALLOT HELPED MAINTAIN THE RADARS AT ALL THREE ANCHORAGE-AREA BATTERIES AND SERVED THERE DURING ***THE '64 EARTHQUAKE.*** HE SPOKE ABOUT THE SITE POINT FIASCO TO THE UNIVERSITY OF ALASKA ORAL HISTORY PROJECT ON ***COLD WAR ALASKA.***

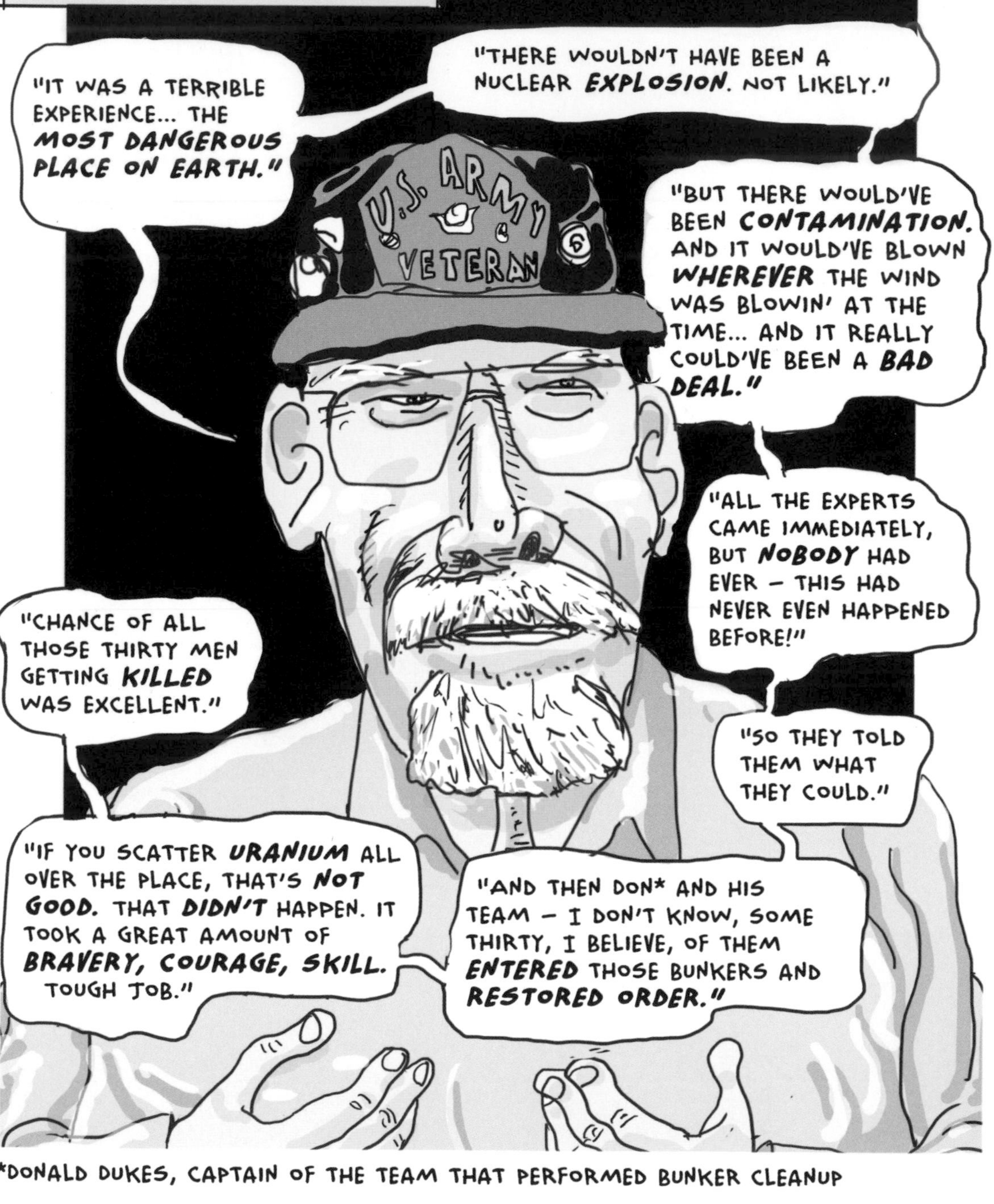
"IT WAS A TERRIBLE EXPERIENCE... THE MOST DANGEROUS PLACE ON EARTH."
"THERE WOULDN'T HAVE BEEN A NUCLEAR EXPLOSION. NOT LIKELY."
"BUT THERE WOULD'VE BEEN CONTAMINATION. AND IT WOULD'VE BLOWN WHEREVER THE WIND WAS BLOWIN' AT THE TIME... AND IT REALLY COULD'VE BEEN A BAD DEAL."
"ALL THE EXPERTS CAME IMMEDIATELY, BUT NOBODY HAD EVER – THIS HAD NEVER EVEN HAPPENED BEFORE!"
"CHANCE OF ALL THOSE THIRTY MEN GETTING KILLED WAS EXCELLENT."
"SO THEY TOLD THEM WHAT THEY COULD."
"IF YOU SCATTER URANIUM ALL OVER THE PLACE, THAT'S NOT GOOD. THAT DIDN'T HAPPEN. IT TOOK A GREAT AMOUNT OF BRAVERY, COURAGE, SKILL. TOUGH JOB."
"AND THEN DON* AND HIS TEAM – I DON'T KNOW, SOME THIRTY, I BELIEVE, OF THEM ENTERED THOSE BUNKERS AND RESTORED ORDER."
U.S. ARMY VETERAN

*DONALD DUKES, CAPTAIN OF THE TEAM THAT PERFORMED BUNKER CLEANUP

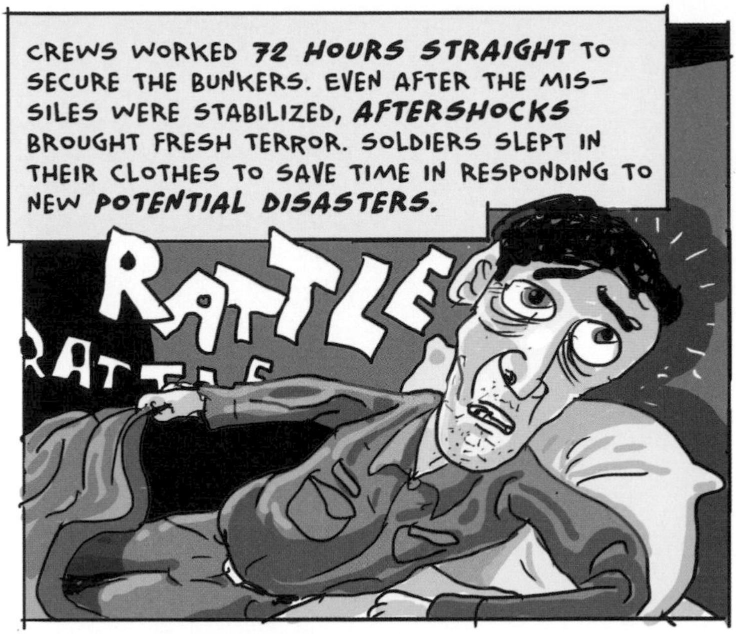
CREWS WORKED 72 HOURS STRAIGHT TO SECURE THE BUNKERS. EVEN AFTER THE MISSILES WERE STABILIZED, AFTERSHOCKS BROUGHT FRESH TERROR. SOLDIERS SLEPT IN THEIR CLOTHES TO SAVE TIME IN RESPONDING TO NEW POTENTIAL DISASTERS.
RATTLE

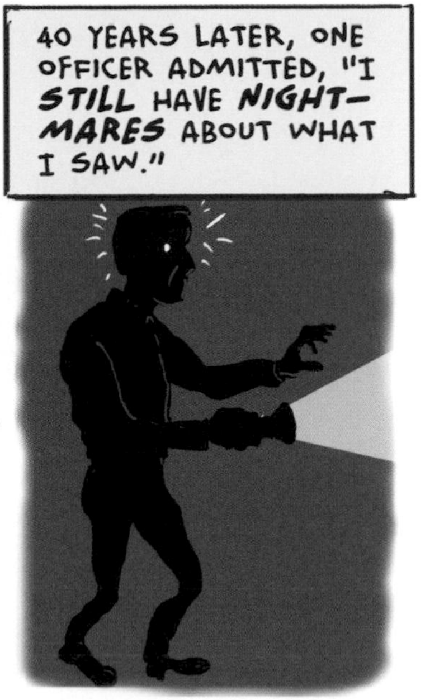
40 YEARS LATER, ONE OFFICER ADMITTED, "I STILL HAVE NIGHTMARES ABOUT WHAT I SAW."

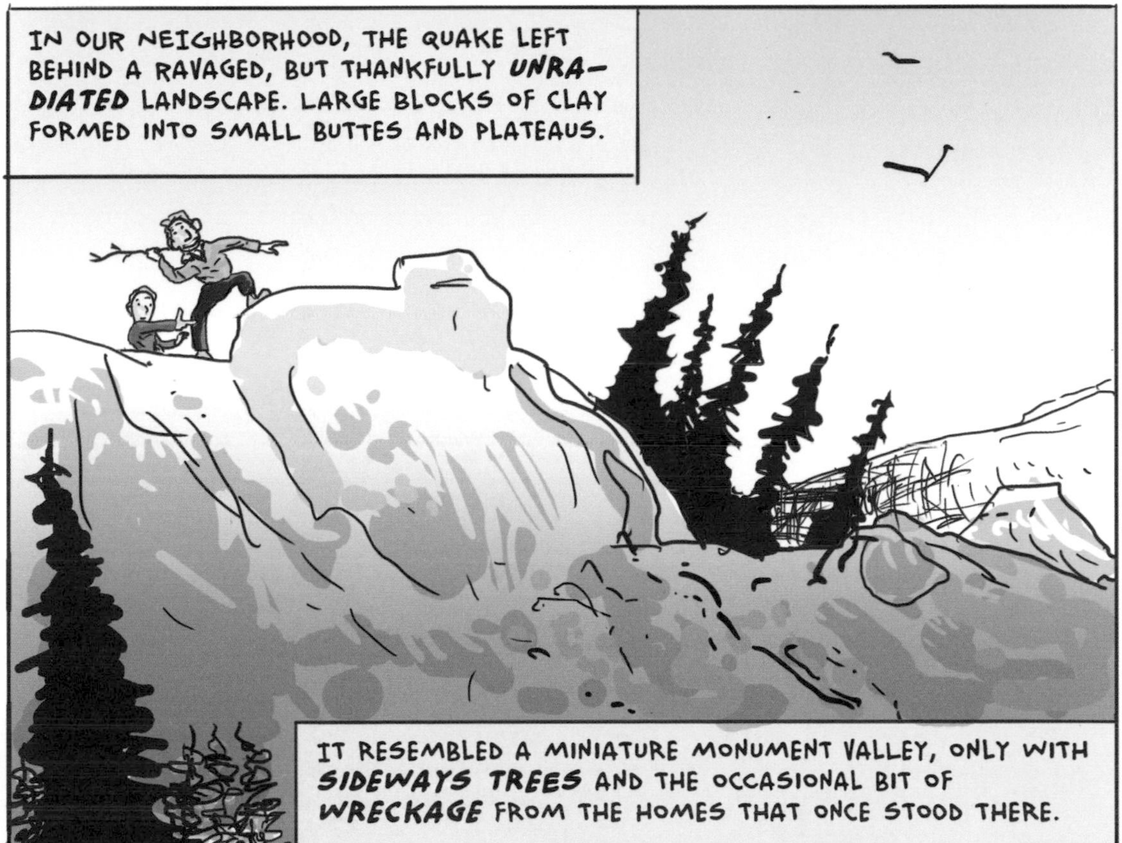
IN OUR NEIGHBORHOOD, THE QUAKE LEFT BEHIND A RAVAGED, BUT THANKFULLY UNRADIATED LANDSCAPE. LARGE BLOCKS OF CLAY FORMED INTO SMALL BUTTES AND PLATEAUS.
IT RESEMBLED A MINIATURE MONUMENT VALLEY, ONLY WITH SIDEWAYS TREES AND THE OCCASIONAL BIT OF WRECKAGE FROM THE HOMES THAT ONCE STOOD THERE.

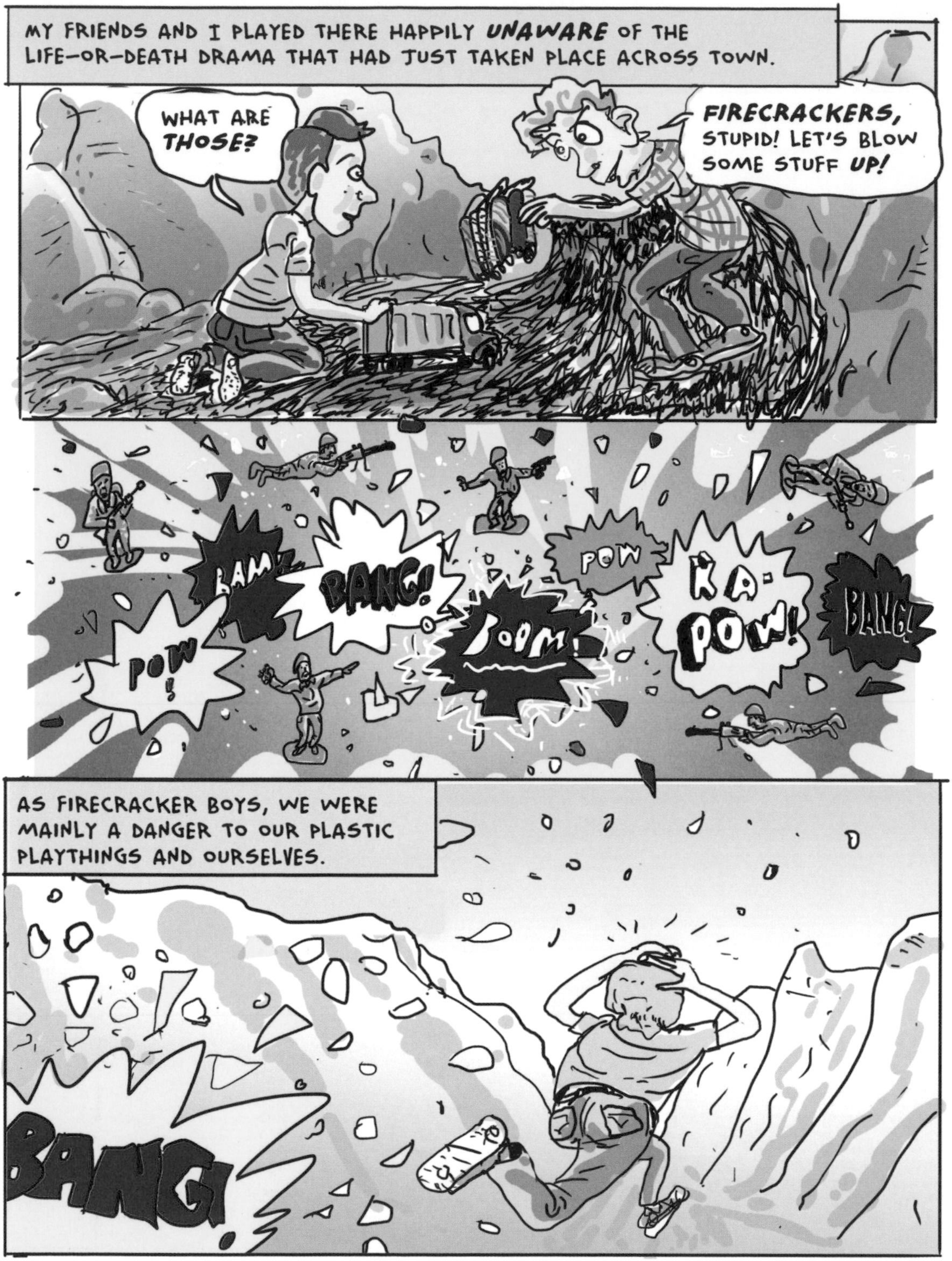
MY FRIENDS AND I PLAYED THERE HAPPILY UNAWARE OF THE LIFE-OR-DEATH DRAMA THAT HAD JUST TAKEN PLACE ACROSS TOWN.
WHAT ARE THOSE?
FIRECRACKERS, STUPID! LET'S BLOW SOME STUFF UP!
BAM!
BANG!
POW
POW!
BOOM!
KA-POW!
BANG!
AS FIRECRACKER BOYS, WE WERE MAINLY A DANGER TO OUR PLASTIC PLAYTHINGS AND OURSELVES.
BANG!

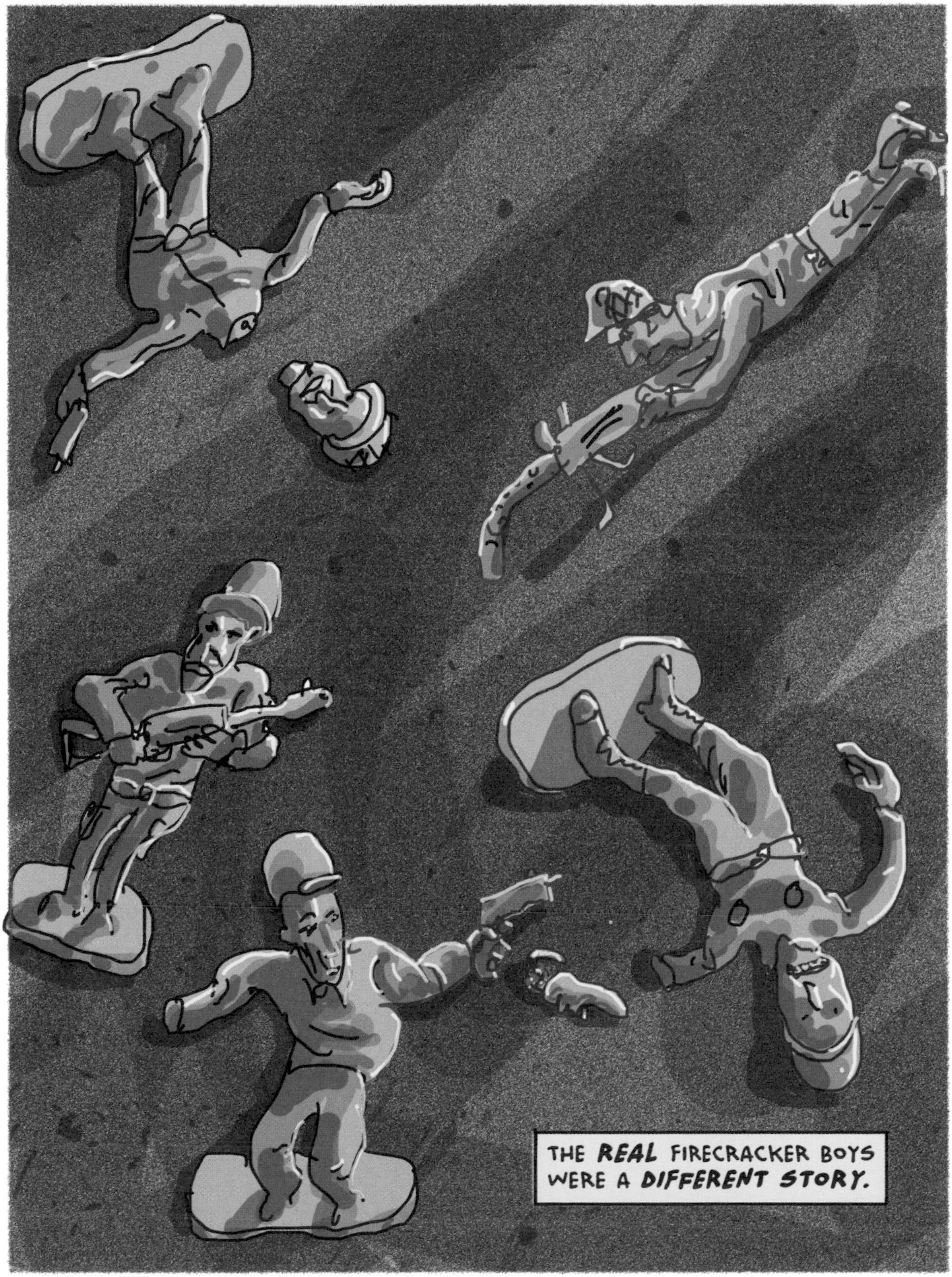
THE REAL FIRECRACKER BOYS
WERE A DIFFERENT STORY.

NUKING ALASKA

2. CHARIOT OF FIRE

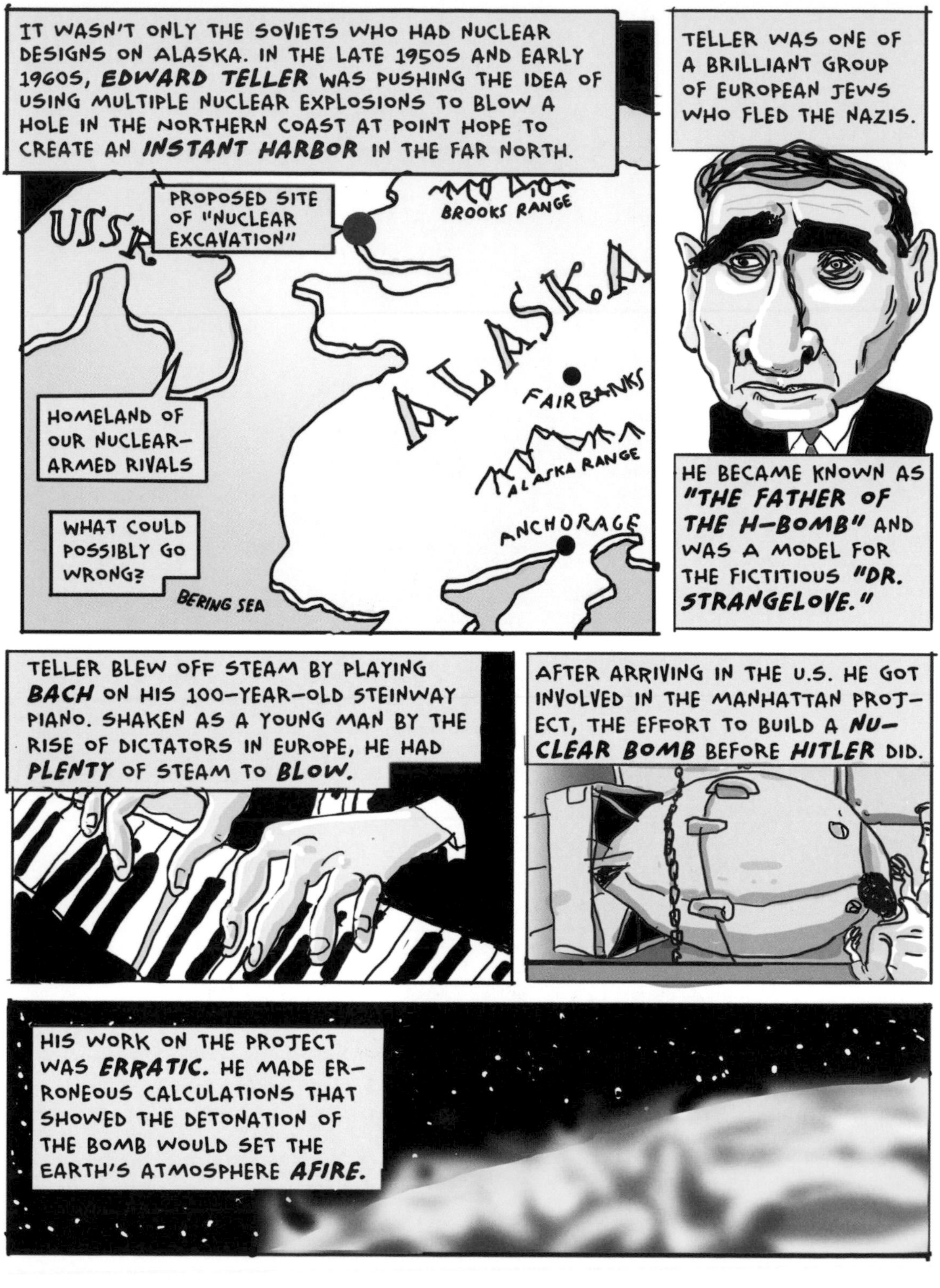
IT WASN'T ONLY THE SOVIETS WHO HAD NUCLEAR DESIGNS ON ALASKA. IN THE LATE 1950S AND EARLY 1960S, EDWARD TELLER WAS PUSHING THE IDEA OF USING MULTIPLE NUCLEAR EXPLOSIONS TO BLOW A HOLE IN THE NORTHERN COAST AT POINT HOPE TO CREATE AN INSTANT HARBOR IN THE FAR NORTH.
USSR
PROPOSED SITE OF "NUCLEAR EXCAVATION"
BROOKS RANGE
ALASKA
FAIRBANKS
ALASKA RANGE
ANCHORAGE
HOMELAND OF OUR NUCLEAR-ARMED RIVALS
WHAT COULD POSSIBLY GO WRONG?
BERING SEA
TELLER WAS ONE OF A BRILLIANT GROUP OF EUROPEAN JEWS WHO FLED THE NAZIS.
HE BECAME KNOWN AS "THE FATHER OF THE H-BOMB" AND WAS A MODEL FOR THE FICTITIOUS "DR. STRANGELOVE."
TELLER BLEW OFF STEAM BY PLAYING BACH ON HIS 100-YEAR-OLD STEINWAY PIANO. SHAKEN AS A YOUNG MAN BY THE RISE OF DICTATORS IN EUROPE, HE HAD PLENTY OF STEAM TO BLOW.
AFTER ARRIVING IN THE U.S. HE GOT INVOLVED IN THE MANHATTAN PROJECT, THE EFFORT TO BUILD A NUCLEAR BOMB BEFORE HITLER DID.
HIS WORK ON THE PROJECT WAS ERRATIC. HE MADE ERRONEOUS CALCULATIONS THAT SHOWED THE DETONATION OF THE BOMB WOULD SET THE EARTH'S ATMOSPHERE AFIRE.

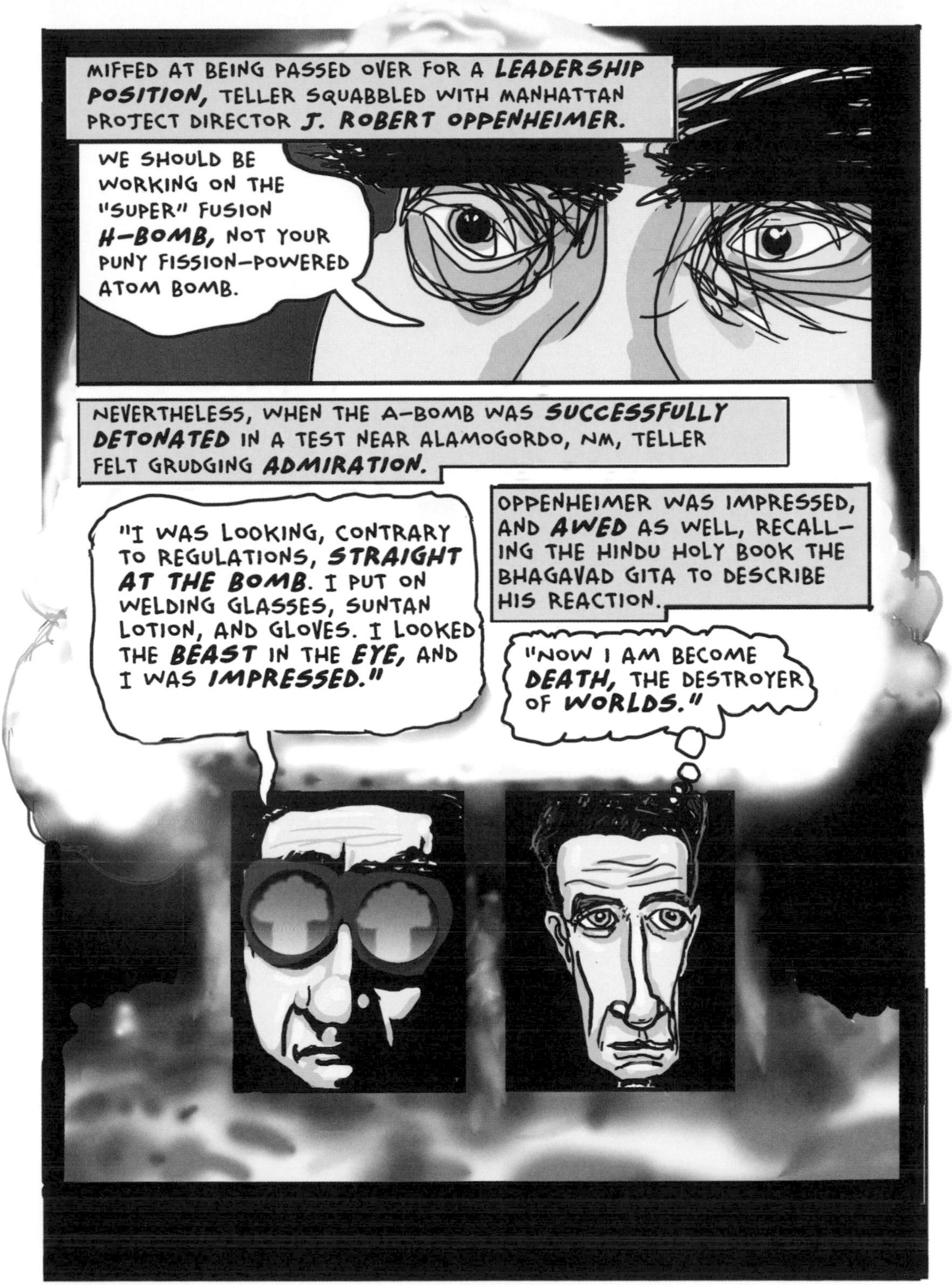

MIFFED AT BEING PASSED OVER FOR A ***LEADERSHIP POSITION,*** TELLER SQUABBLED WITH MANHATTAN PROJECT DIRECTOR ***J. ROBERT OPPENHEIMER.***
WE SHOULD BE WORKING ON THE "SUPER" FUSION ***H-BOMB,*** NOT YOUR PUNY FISSION-POWERED ATOM BOMB.
NEVERTHELESS, WHEN THE A-BOMB WAS ***SUCCESSFULLY DETONATED*** IN A TEST NEAR ALAMOGORDO, NM, TELLER FELT GRUDGING ***ADMIRATION.***
"I WAS LOOKING, CONTRARY TO REGULATIONS, ***STRAIGHT AT THE BOMB***. I PUT ON WELDING GLASSES, SUNTAN LOTION, AND GLOVES. I LOOKED THE ***BEAST*** IN THE ***EYE,*** AND I WAS ***IMPRESSED.***"
OPPENHEIMER WAS IMPRESSED, AND ***AWED*** AS WELL, RECALLING THE HINDU HOLY BOOK THE BHAGAVAD GITA TO DESCRIBE HIS REACTION.
"NOW I AM BECOME ***DEATH,*** THE DESTROYER OF ***WORLDS.***"

TELLER PURSUED DEVELOPMENT OF THE *"SUPER BOMB"* AFTER WWII, CONVINCED IT WAS CRITICAL FOR THE WEST'S *SURVIVAL* OF THE *COLD WAR.*

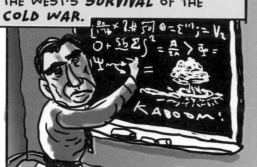

IN A WAY, THE H-BOMB EXISTS IN *SPITE* OF TELLER. HIS EARLY DESIGN WAS *FLAWED.* IT WAS CORRECTED BY STANISLAW ULAM.

HE'S GOT MY EYES...

BUT TELLER GOT THE PATERNITY RIGHTS.

DURING THE COLD WAR, TELLER FOR-SOOK PHYSICS TO BECOME A *SCIENCE ADVISOR* TO PRESIDENTS. THROUGH THE REAGAN YEARS, HE PUSHED *NUCLEAR ENERGY* AND *WEAPONS.*

WORRIED OVER THE BAD P.R. HAUNT-ING THE NUCLEAR BRAND, TELLER SOUGHT PEACEFUL WAYS TO *REHA-BILITATE* THE BOMB'S *IMAGE.*

EXTRACT OIL FROM ALBERTA TAR SANDS?

ASTEROID IMPACT AVOIDANCE?

IN HIS CAPACITY AS HEAD OF THE LAWRENCE LIVERMORE LAB, HE USED HIS INFLUENCE TO *ADVOCATE* FOR *HUGE ATOMIC PROJECTS.*

INSTANT HARBOR!

TELLER AND THE ATOMIC ENERGY COMMIS-SION CAME UP WITH THE IDEA OF CREATING A HARBOR WITH NUCLEAR BLASTS. BUT *WHERE* COULD THEY *PUT* THE HARBOR?

WE NEED SOMEPLACE REMOTE, WHERE PEOPLE ARE FEW...

ALASKA!

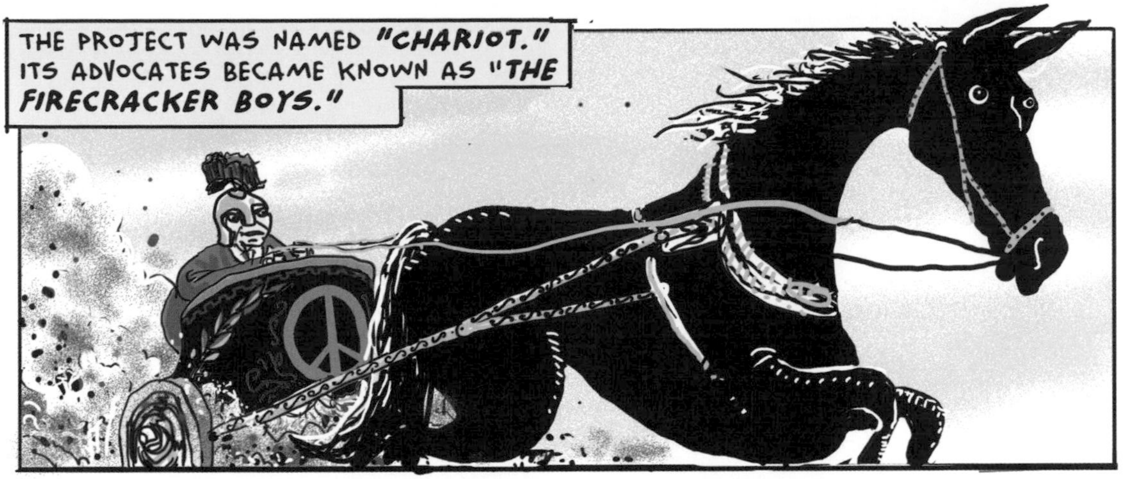
THE PROJECT WAS NAMED "CHARIOT." ITS ADVOCATES BECAME KNOWN AS "THE FIRECRACKER BOYS."

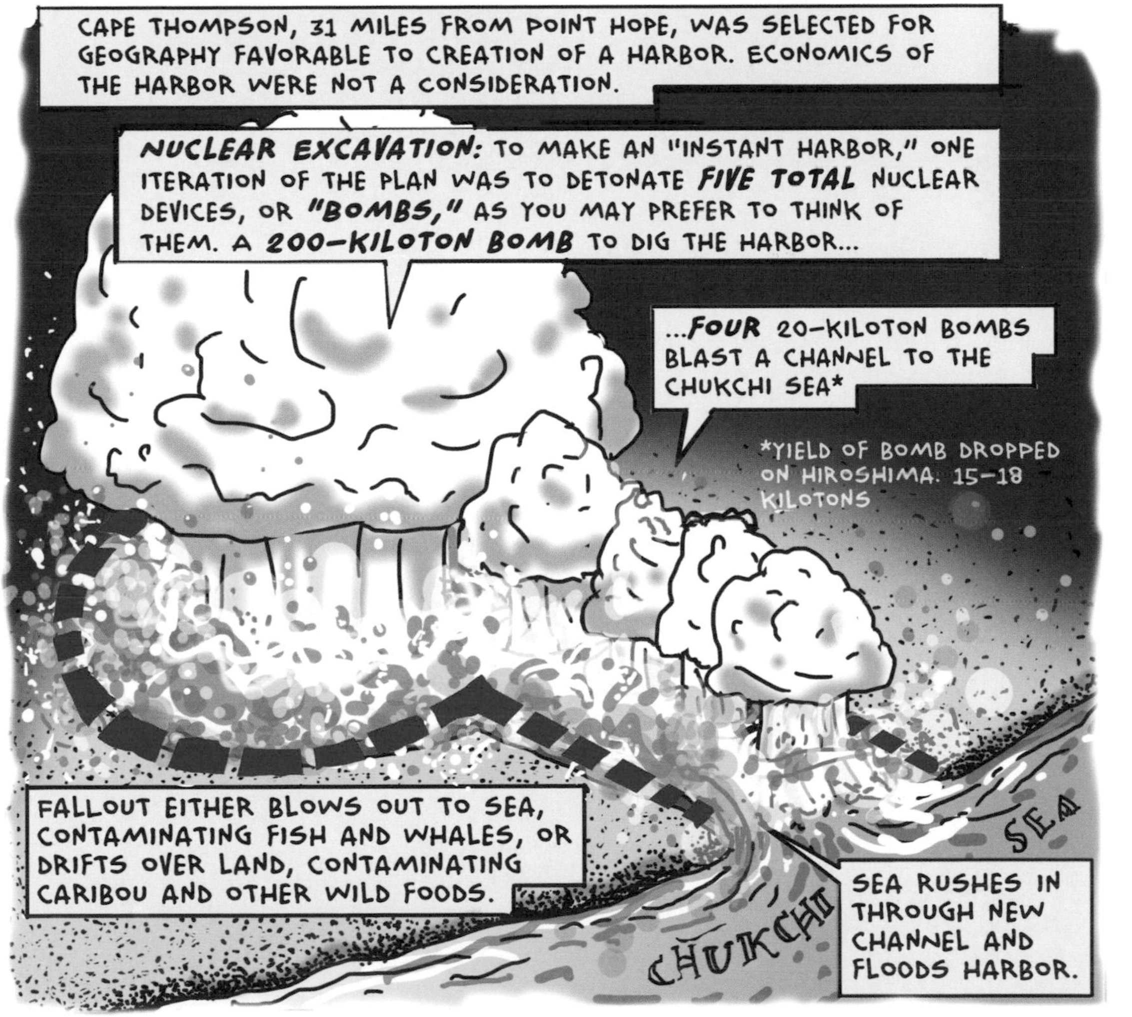
CAPE THOMPSON, 31 MILES FROM POINT HOPE, WAS SELECTED FOR GEOGRAPHY FAVORABLE TO CREATION OF A HARBOR. ECONOMICS OF THE HARBOR WERE NOT A CONSIDERATION.
NUCLEAR EXCAVATION: TO MAKE AN "INSTANT HARBOR," ONE ITERATION OF THE PLAN WAS TO DETONATE FIVE TOTAL NUCLEAR DEVICES, OR "BOMBS," AS YOU MAY PREFER TO THINK OF THEM. A 200-KILOTON BOMB TO DIG THE HARBOR...
...FOUR 20-KILOTON BOMBS BLAST A CHANNEL TO THE CHUKCHI SEA*
*YIELD OF BOMB DROPPED ON HIROSHIMA: 15-18 KILOTONS
FALLOUT EITHER BLOWS OUT TO SEA, CONTAMINATING FISH AND WHALES, OR DRIFTS OVER LAND, CONTAMINATING CARIBOU AND OTHER WILD FOODS.
CHUKCHI SEA
SEA RUSHES IN THROUGH NEW CHANNEL AND FLOODS HARBOR.

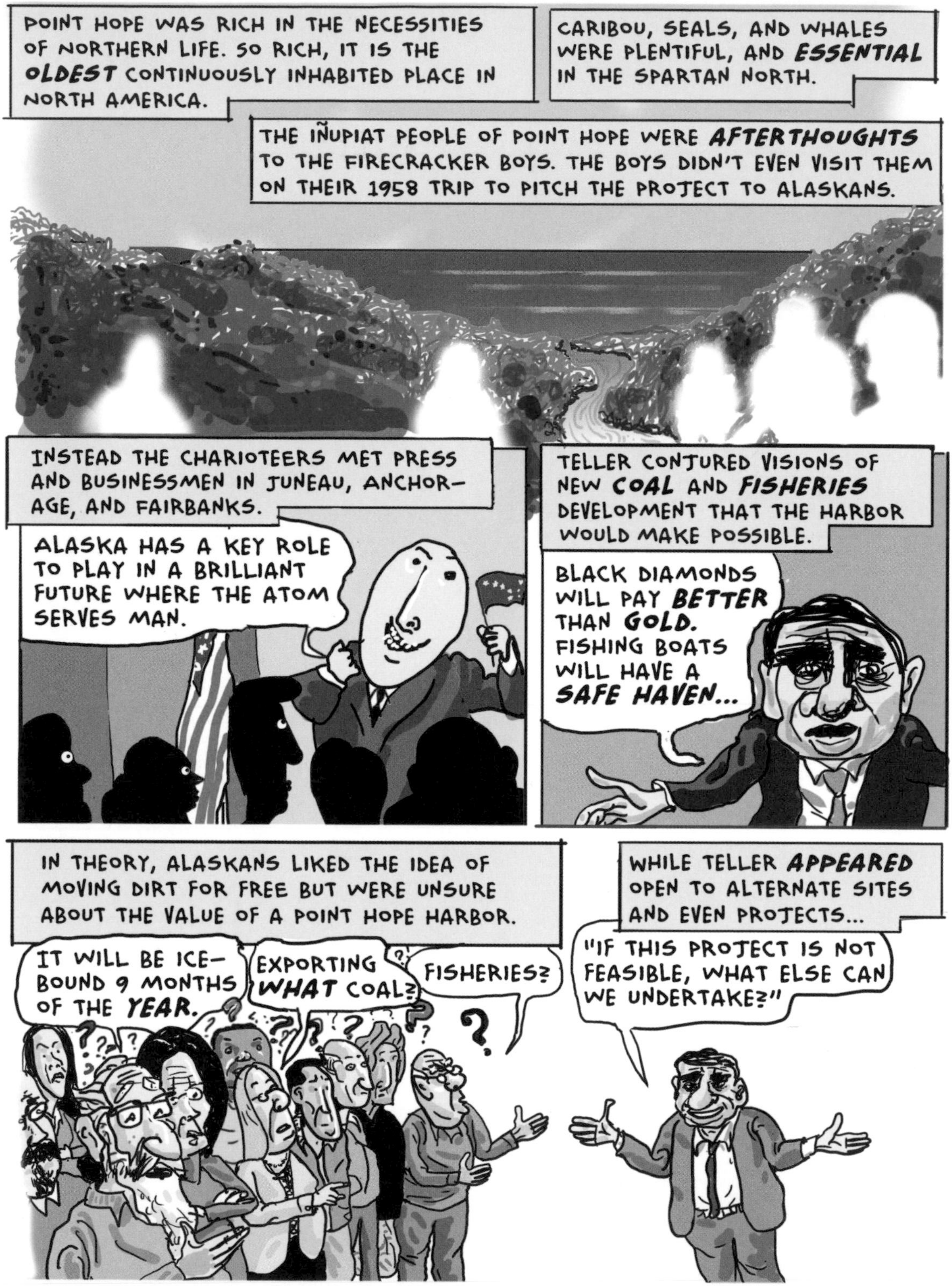
POINT HOPE WAS RICH IN THE NECESSITIES OF NORTHERN LIFE. SO RICH, IT IS THE *OLDEST* CONTINUOUSLY INHABITED PLACE IN NORTH AMERICA.
CARIBOU, SEALS, AND WHALES WERE PLENTIFUL, AND *ESSENTIAL* IN THE SPARTAN NORTH.
THE IÑUPIAT PEOPLE OF POINT HOPE WERE *AFTERTHOUGHTS* TO THE FIRECRACKER BOYS. THE BOYS DIDN'T EVEN VISIT THEM ON THEIR 1958 TRIP TO PITCH THE PROJECT TO ALASKANS.
INSTEAD THE CHARIOTEERS MET PRESS AND BUSINESSMEN IN JUNEAU, ANCHORAGE, AND FAIRBANKS.
ALASKA HAS A KEY ROLE TO PLAY IN A BRILLIANT FUTURE WHERE THE ATOM SERVES MAN.
TELLER CONJURED VISIONS OF NEW *COAL* AND *FISHERIES* DEVELOPMENT THAT THE HARBOR WOULD MAKE POSSIBLE.
BLACK DIAMONDS WILL PAY *BETTER* THAN *GOLD.* FISHING BOATS WILL HAVE A *SAFE HAVEN...*
IN THEORY, ALASKANS LIKED THE IDEA OF MOVING DIRT FOR FREE BUT WERE UNSURE ABOUT THE VALUE OF A POINT HOPE HARBOR.
IT WILL BE ICE-BOUND 9 MONTHS OF THE *YEAR.*
EXPORTING *WHAT* COAL?
FISHERIES?
WHILE TELLER *APPEARED* OPEN TO ALTERNATE SITES AND EVEN PROJECTS...
"IF THIS PROJECT IS NOT FEASIBLE, WHAT ELSE CAN WE UNDERTAKE?"

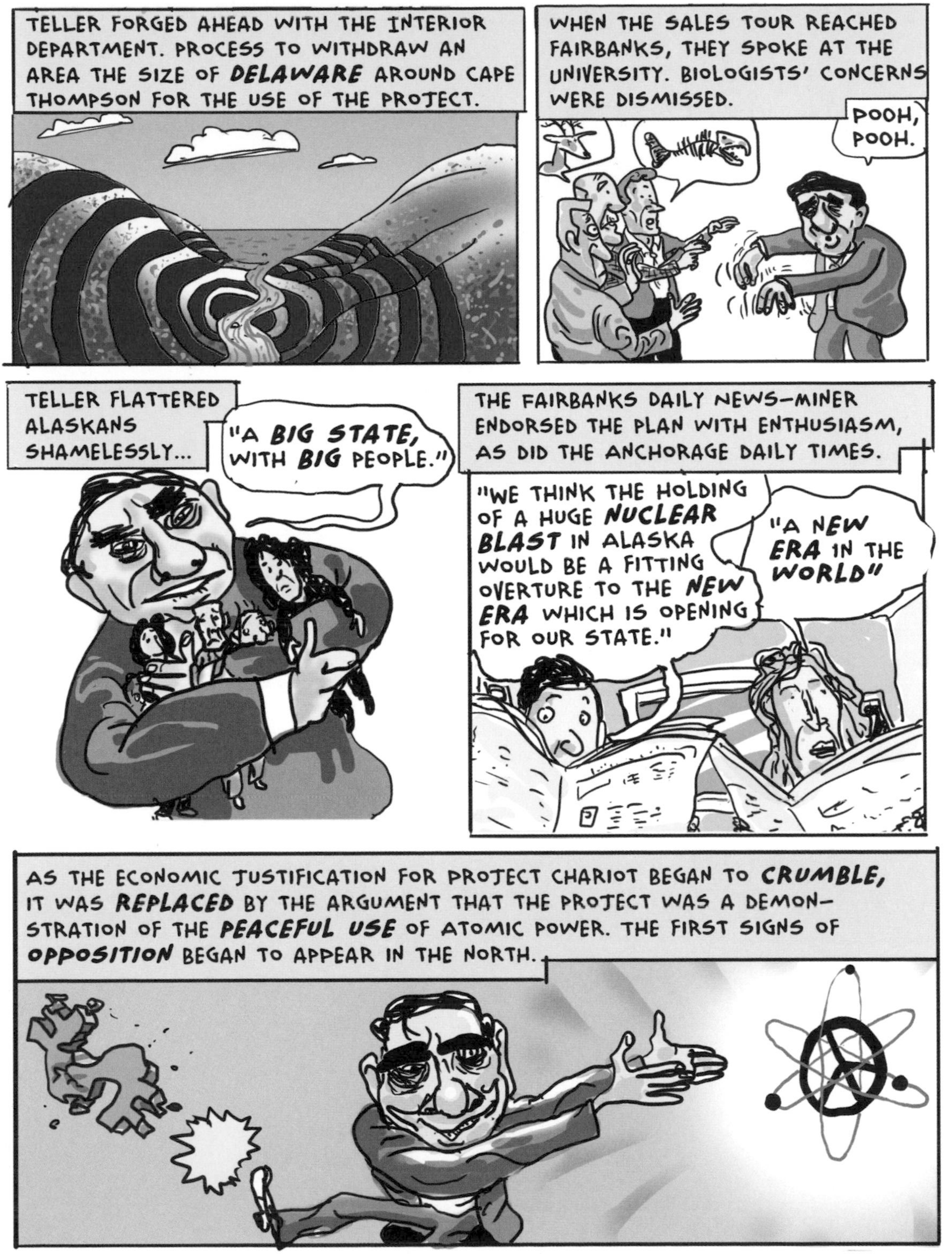
TELLER FORGED AHEAD WITH THE INTERIOR DEPARTMENT. PROCESS TO WITHDRAW AN AREA THE SIZE OF DELAWARE AROUND CAPE THOMPSON FOR THE USE OF THE PROJECT.
WHEN THE SALES TOUR REACHED FAIRBANKS, THEY SPOKE AT THE UNIVERSITY. BIOLOGISTS' CONCERNS WERE DISMISSED.
POOH, POOH.
TELLER FLATTERED ALASKANS SHAMELESSLY...
"A BIG STATE, WITH BIG PEOPLE."
THE FAIRBANKS DAILY NEWS-MINER ENDORSED THE PLAN WITH ENTHUSIASM, AS DID THE ANCHORAGE DAILY TIMES.
"WE THINK THE HOLDING OF A HUGE NUCLEAR BLAST IN ALASKA WOULD BE A FITTING OVERTURE TO THE NEW ERA WHICH IS OPENING FOR OUR STATE."
"A NEW ERA IN THE WORLD"
AS THE ECONOMIC JUSTIFICATION FOR PROJECT CHARIOT BEGAN TO CRUMBLE, IT WAS REPLACED BY THE ARGUMENT THAT THE PROJECT WAS A DEMONSTRATION OF THE PEACEFUL USE OF ATOMIC POWER. THE FIRST SIGNS OF OPPOSITION BEGAN TO APPEAR IN THE NORTH.

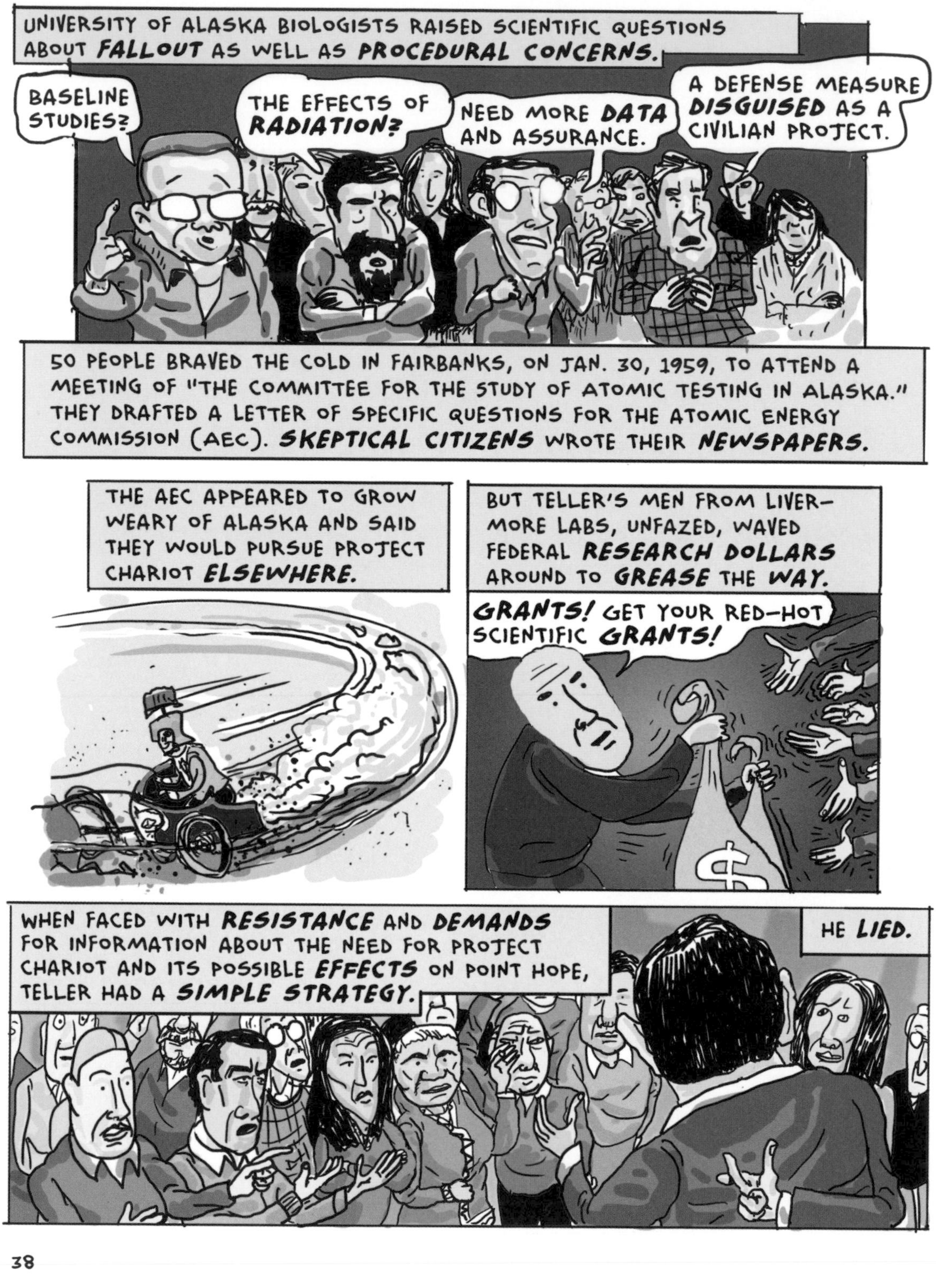
UNIVERSITY OF ALASKA BIOLOGISTS RAISED SCIENTIFIC QUESTIONS ABOUT FALLOUT AS WELL AS PROCEDURAL CONCERNS.
BASELINE STUDIES?
THE EFFECTS OF RADIATION?
NEED MORE DATA AND ASSURANCE.
A DEFENSE MEASURE DISGUISED AS A CIVILIAN PROJECT.
50 PEOPLE BRAVED THE COLD IN FAIRBANKS, ON JAN. 30, 1959, TO ATTEND A MEETING OF "THE COMMITTEE FOR THE STUDY OF ATOMIC TESTING IN ALASKA." THEY DRAFTED A LETTER OF SPECIFIC QUESTIONS FOR THE ATOMIC ENERGY COMMISSION (AEC). SKEPTICAL CITIZENS WROTE THEIR NEWSPAPERS.
THE AEC APPEARED TO GROW WEARY OF ALASKA AND SAID THEY WOULD PURSUE PROJECT CHARIOT ELSEWHERE.
BUT TELLER'S MEN FROM LIVERMORE LABS, UNFAZED, WAVED FEDERAL RESEARCH DOLLARS AROUND TO GREASE THE WAY.
GRANTS! GET YOUR RED-HOT SCIENTIFIC GRANTS!
$
WHEN FACED WITH RESISTANCE AND DEMANDS FOR INFORMATION ABOUT THE NEED FOR PROJECT CHARIOT AND ITS POSSIBLE EFFECTS ON POINT HOPE, TELLER HAD A SIMPLE STRATEGY.
HE LIED.

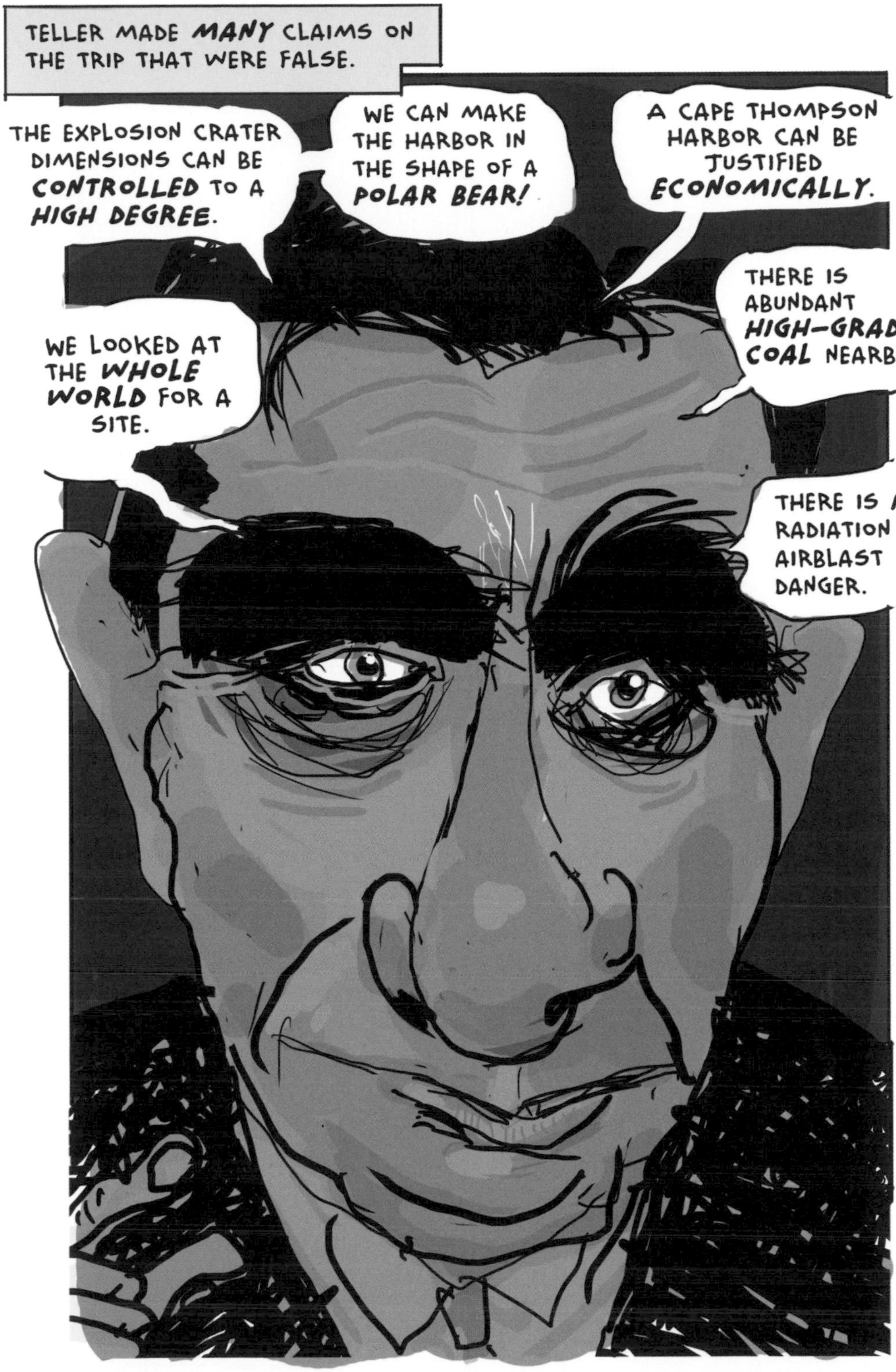
TELLER MADE MANY CLAIMS ON THE TRIP THAT WERE FALSE.
THE EXPLOSION CRATER DIMENSIONS CAN BE CONTROLLED TO A HIGH DEGREE.
WE CAN MAKE THE HARBOR IN THE SHAPE OF A POLAR BEAR!
A CAPE THOMPSON HARBOR CAN BE JUSTIFIED ECONOMICALLY.
THERE IS ABUNDANT HIGH-GRADE COAL NEARBY.
WE LOOKED AT THE WHOLE WORLD FOR A SITE.
THERE IS NO RADIATION OR AIRBLAST DANGER.

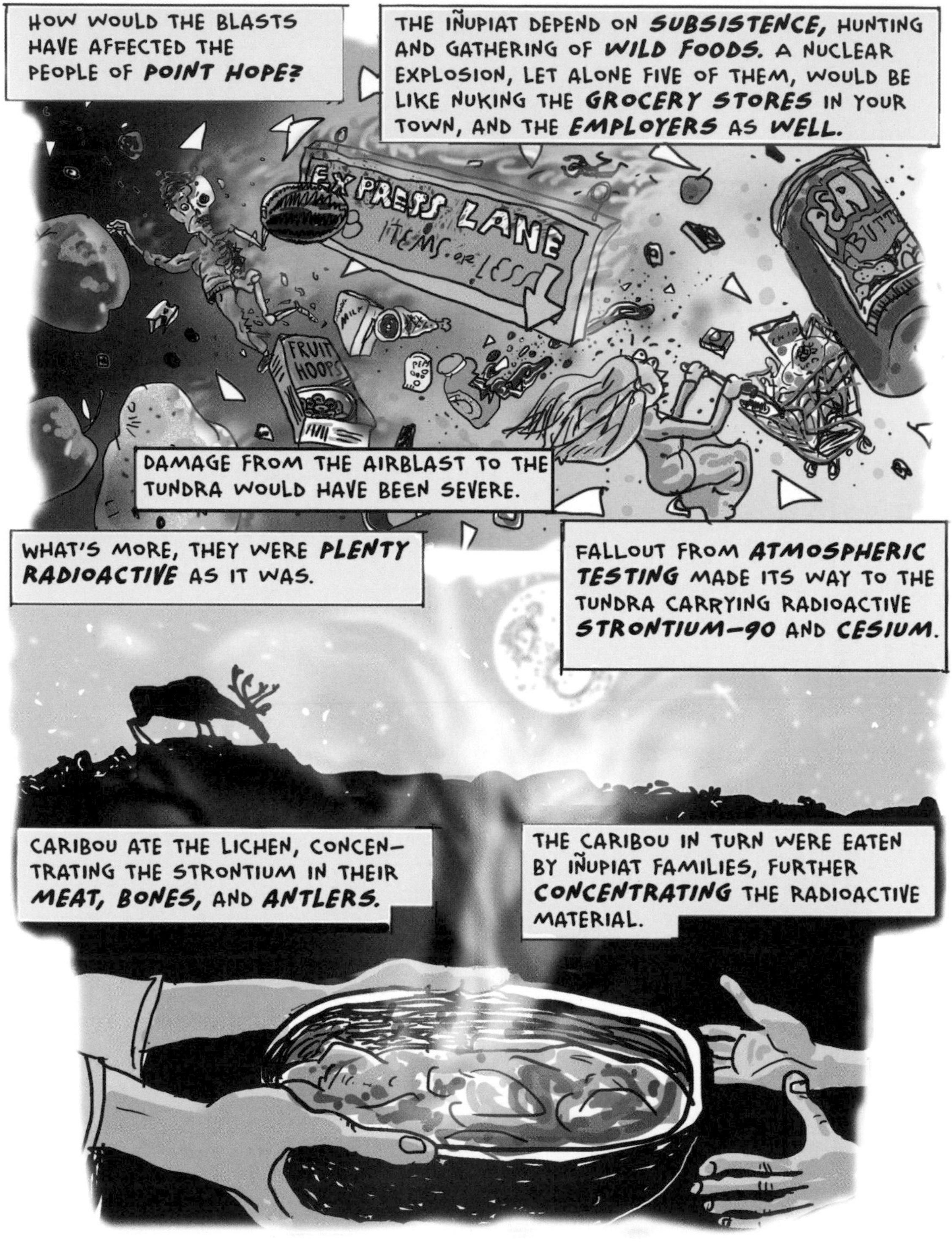
HOW WOULD THE BLASTS HAVE AFFECTED THE PEOPLE OF POINT HOPE?
THE IÑUPIAT DEPEND ON SUBSISTENCE, HUNTING AND GATHERING OF WILD FOODS. A NUCLEAR EXPLOSION, LET ALONE FIVE OF THEM, WOULD BE LIKE NUKING THE GROCERY STORES IN YOUR TOWN, AND THE EMPLOYERS AS WELL.
EXPRESS LANE
ITEMS OR LESS
FRUIT HOOPS
DAMAGE FROM THE AIRBLAST TO THE TUNDRA WOULD HAVE BEEN SEVERE.
WHAT'S MORE, THEY WERE PLENTY RADIOACTIVE AS IT WAS.
FALLOUT FROM ATMOSPHERIC TESTING MADE ITS WAY TO THE TUNDRA CARRYING RADIOACTIVE STRONTIUM-90 AND CESIUM.
CARIBOU ATE THE LICHEN, CONCENTRATING THE STRONTIUM IN THEIR MEAT, BONES, AND ANTLERS.
THE CARIBOU IN TURN WERE EATEN BY IÑUPIAT FAMILIES, FURTHER CONCENTRATING THE RADIOACTIVE MATERIAL.

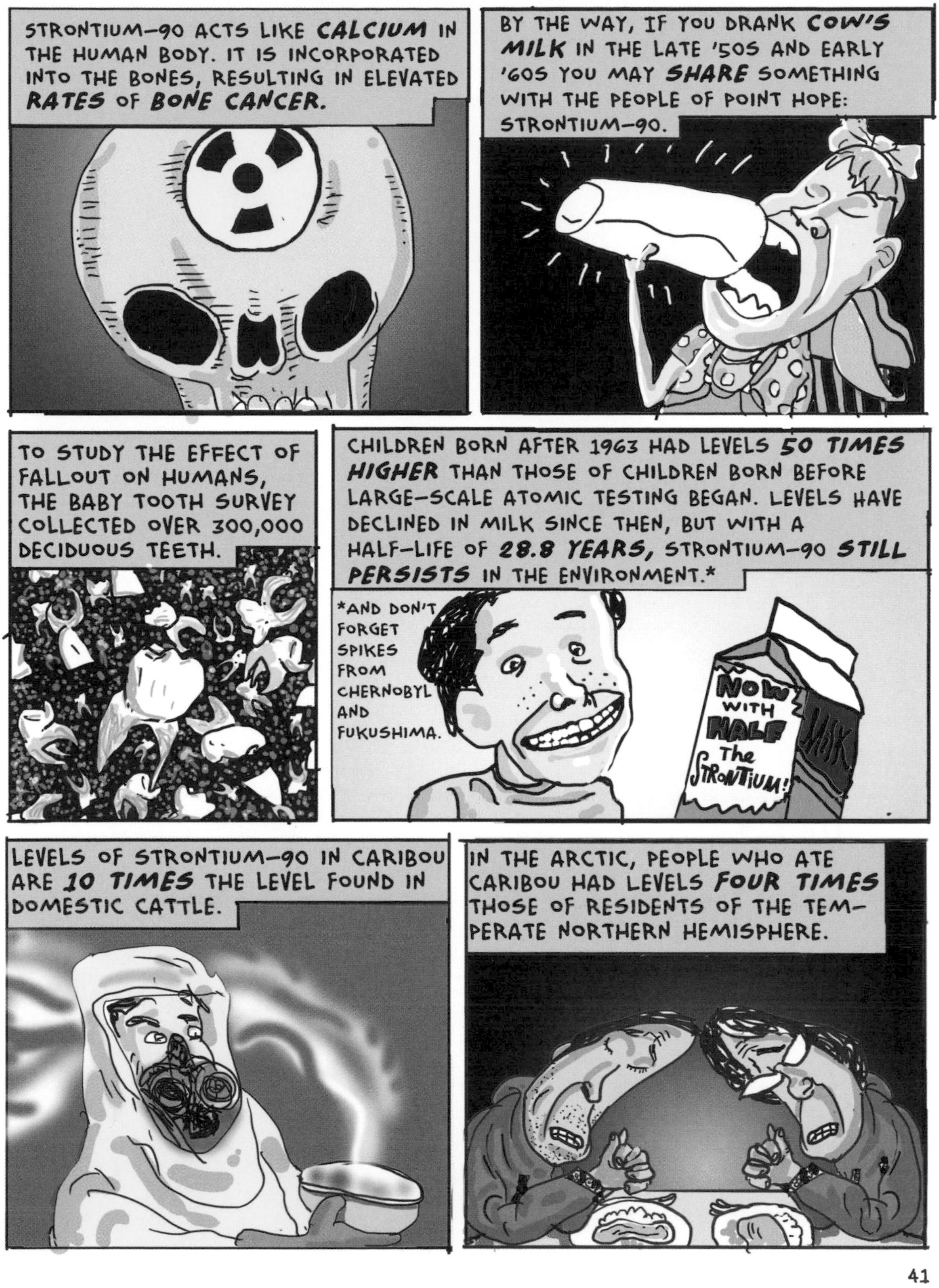
STRONTIUM-90 ACTS LIKE CALCIUM IN THE HUMAN BODY. IT IS INCORPORATED INTO THE BONES, RESULTING IN ELEVATED RATES OF BONE CANCER.
BY THE WAY, IF YOU DRANK COW'S MILK IN THE LATE '50S AND EARLY '60S YOU MAY SHARE SOMETHING WITH THE PEOPLE OF POINT HOPE: STRONTIUM-90.
TO STUDY THE EFFECT OF FALLOUT ON HUMANS, THE BABY TOOTH SURVEY COLLECTED OVER 300,000 DECIDUOUS TEETH.
CHILDREN BORN AFTER 1963 HAD LEVELS 50 TIMES HIGHER THAN THOSE OF CHILDREN BORN BEFORE LARGE-SCALE ATOMIC TESTING BEGAN. LEVELS HAVE DECLINED IN MILK SINCE THEN, BUT WITH A HALF-LIFE OF 28.8 YEARS, STRONTIUM-90 STILL PERSISTS IN THE ENVIRONMENT.*
*AND DON'T FORGET SPIKES FROM CHERNOBYL AND FUKUSHIMA.
NOW WITH HALF The STRONTIUM!
MILK
LEVELS OF STRONTIUM-90 IN CARIBOU ARE 10 TIMES THE LEVEL FOUND IN DOMESTIC CATTLE.
IN THE ARCTIC, PEOPLE WHO ATE CARIBOU HAD LEVELS FOUR TIMES THOSE OF RESIDENTS OF THE TEMPERATE NORTHERN HEMISPHERE.

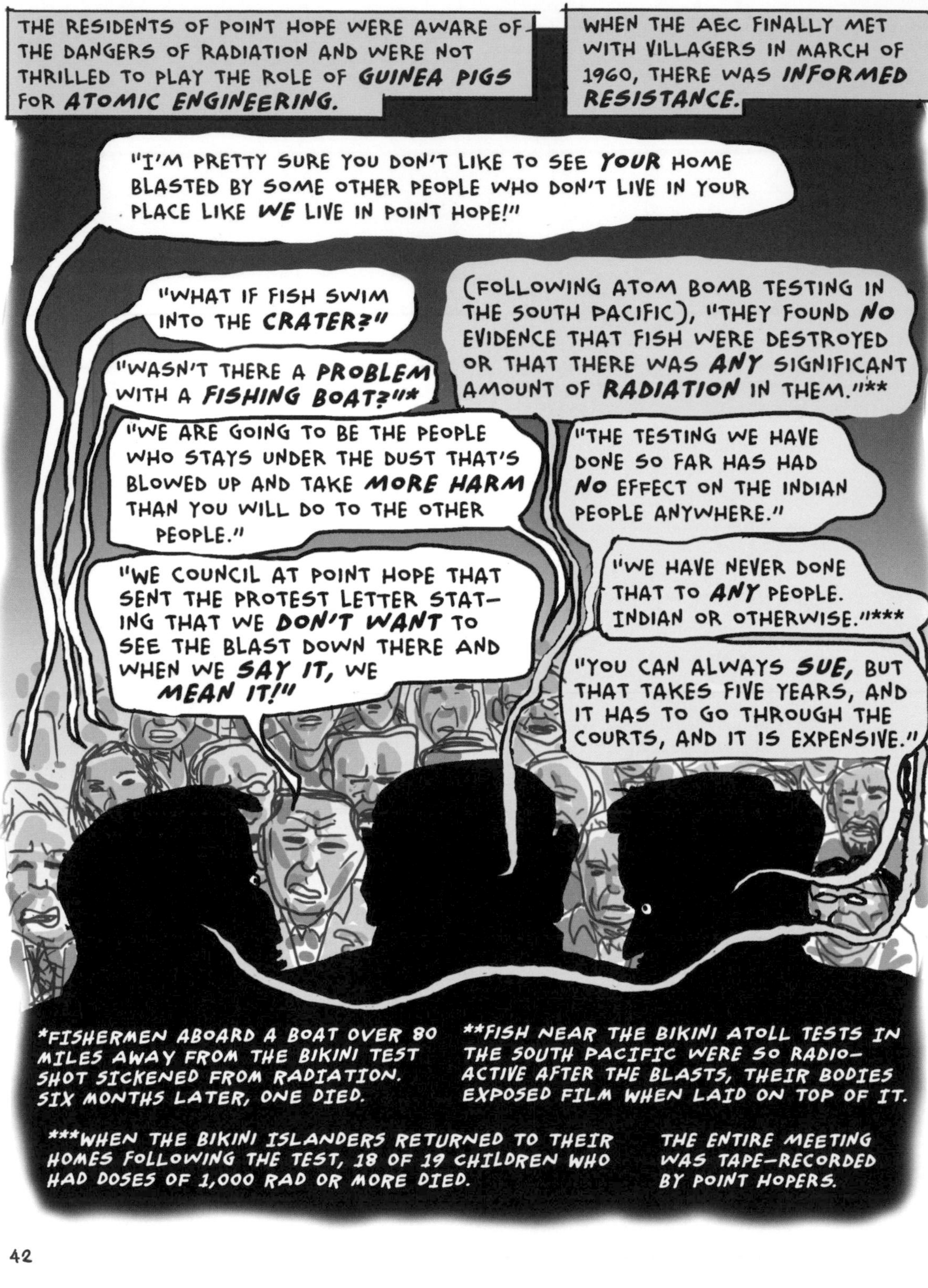
THE RESIDENTS OF POINT HOPE WERE AWARE OF THE DANGERS OF RADIATION AND WERE NOT THRILLED TO PLAY THE ROLE OF *GUINEA PIGS* FOR *ATOMIC ENGINEERING.*
WHEN THE AEC FINALLY MET WITH VILLAGERS IN MARCH OF 1960, THERE WAS *INFORMED RESISTANCE.*
"I'M PRETTY SURE YOU DON'T LIKE TO SEE *YOUR* HOME BLASTED BY SOME OTHER PEOPLE WHO DON'T LIVE IN YOUR PLACE LIKE *WE* LIVE IN POINT HOPE!"
"WHAT IF FISH SWIM INTO THE *CRATER?*"
"WASN'T THERE A *PROBLEM* WITH A *FISHING BOAT?*"*
"WE ARE GOING TO BE THE PEOPLE WHO STAYS UNDER THE DUST THAT'S BLOWED UP AND TAKE *MORE HARM* THAN YOU WILL DO TO THE OTHER PEOPLE."
"WE COUNCIL AT POINT HOPE THAT SENT THE PROTEST LETTER STATING THAT WE *DON'T WANT* TO SEE THE BLAST DOWN THERE AND WHEN WE *SAY IT,* WE *MEAN IT!*"
(FOLLOWING ATOM BOMB TESTING IN THE SOUTH PACIFIC), "THEY FOUND *NO* EVIDENCE THAT FISH WERE DESTROYED OR THAT THERE WAS *ANY* SIGNIFICANT AMOUNT OF *RADIATION* IN THEM."**
"THE TESTING WE HAVE DONE SO FAR HAS HAD *NO* EFFECT ON THE INDIAN PEOPLE ANYWHERE."
"WE HAVE NEVER DONE THAT TO *ANY* PEOPLE. INDIAN OR OTHERWISE."***
"YOU CAN ALWAYS *SUE,* BUT THAT TAKES FIVE YEARS, AND IT HAS TO GO THROUGH THE COURTS, AND IT IS EXPENSIVE."
*FISHERMEN ABOARD A BOAT OVER 80 MILES AWAY FROM THE BIKINI TEST SHOT SICKENED FROM RADIATION. SIX MONTHS LATER, ONE DIED.
**FISH NEAR THE BIKINI ATOLL TESTS IN THE SOUTH PACIFIC WERE SO RADIOACTIVE AFTER THE BLASTS, THEIR BODIES EXPOSED FILM WHEN LAID ON TOP OF IT.
***WHEN THE BIKINI ISLANDERS RETURNED TO THEIR HOMES FOLLOWING THE TEST, 18 OF 19 CHILDREN WHO HAD DOSES OF 1,000 RAD OR MORE DIED.
THE ENTIRE MEETING WAS TAPE-RECORDED BY POINT HOPERS.

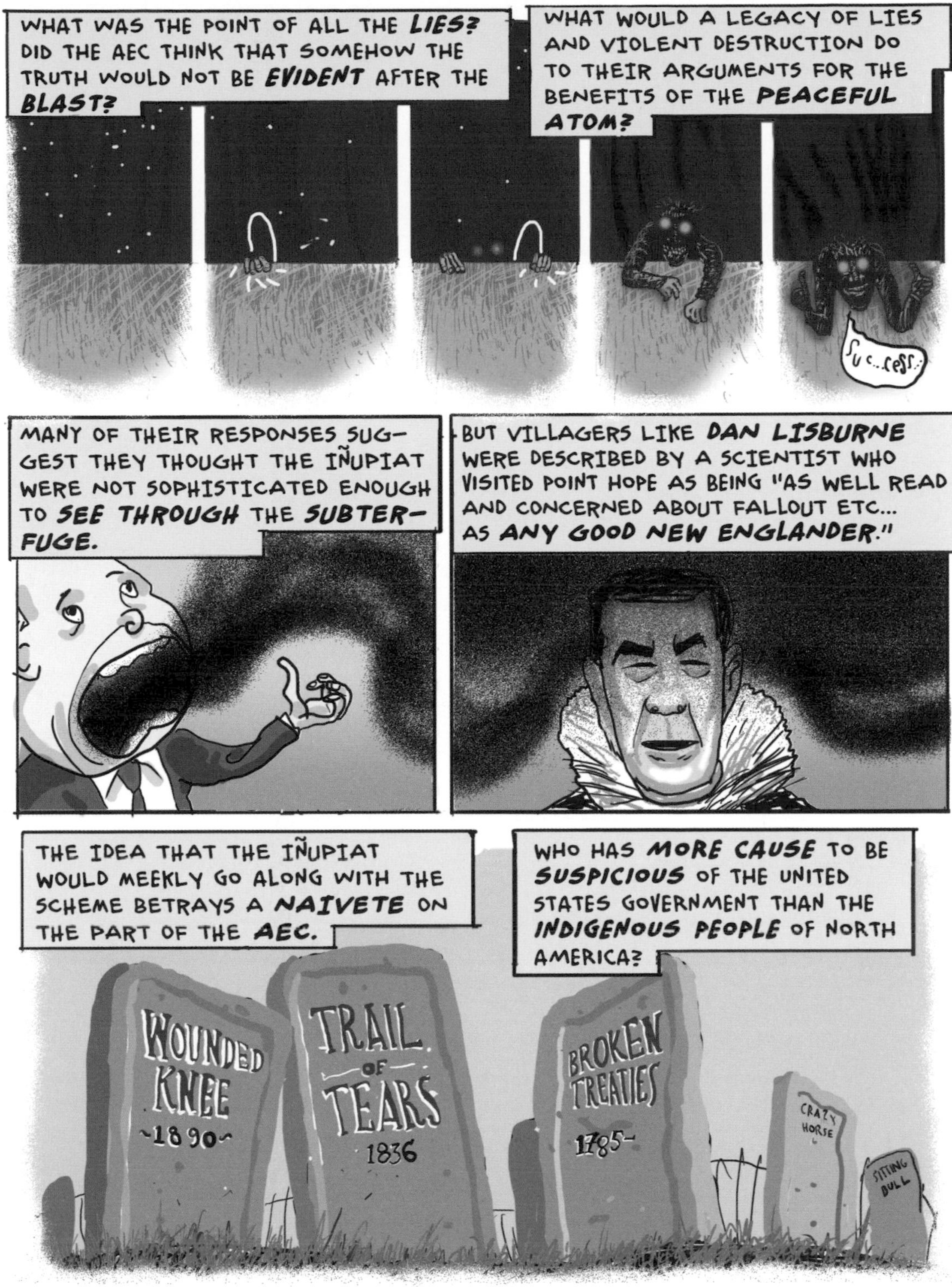
WHAT WAS THE POINT OF ALL THE LIES? DID THE AEC THINK THAT SOMEHOW THE TRUTH WOULD NOT BE EVIDENT AFTER THE BLAST?
WHAT WOULD A LEGACY OF LIES AND VIOLENT DESTRUCTION DO TO THEIR ARGUMENTS FOR THE BENEFITS OF THE PEACEFUL ATOM?
SUC...CESS...
MANY OF THEIR RESPONSES SUGGEST THEY THOUGHT THE IÑUPIAT WERE NOT SOPHISTICATED ENOUGH TO SEE THROUGH THE SUBTERFUGE.
BUT VILLAGERS LIKE DAN LISBURNE WERE DESCRIBED BY A SCIENTIST WHO VISITED POINT HOPE AS BEING "AS WELL READ AND CONCERNED ABOUT FALLOUT ETC... AS ANY GOOD NEW ENGLANDER."
THE IDEA THAT THE IÑUPIAT WOULD MEEKLY GO ALONG WITH THE SCHEME BETRAYS A NAIVETE ON THE PART OF THE AEC.
WHO HAS MORE CAUSE TO BE SUSPICIOUS OF THE UNITED STATES GOVERNMENT THAN THE INDIGENOUS PEOPLE OF NORTH AMERICA?
WOUNDED KNEE ~1890~
TRAIL OF TEARS 1836
BROKEN TREATIES 1785
CRAZY HORSE
SITTING BULL

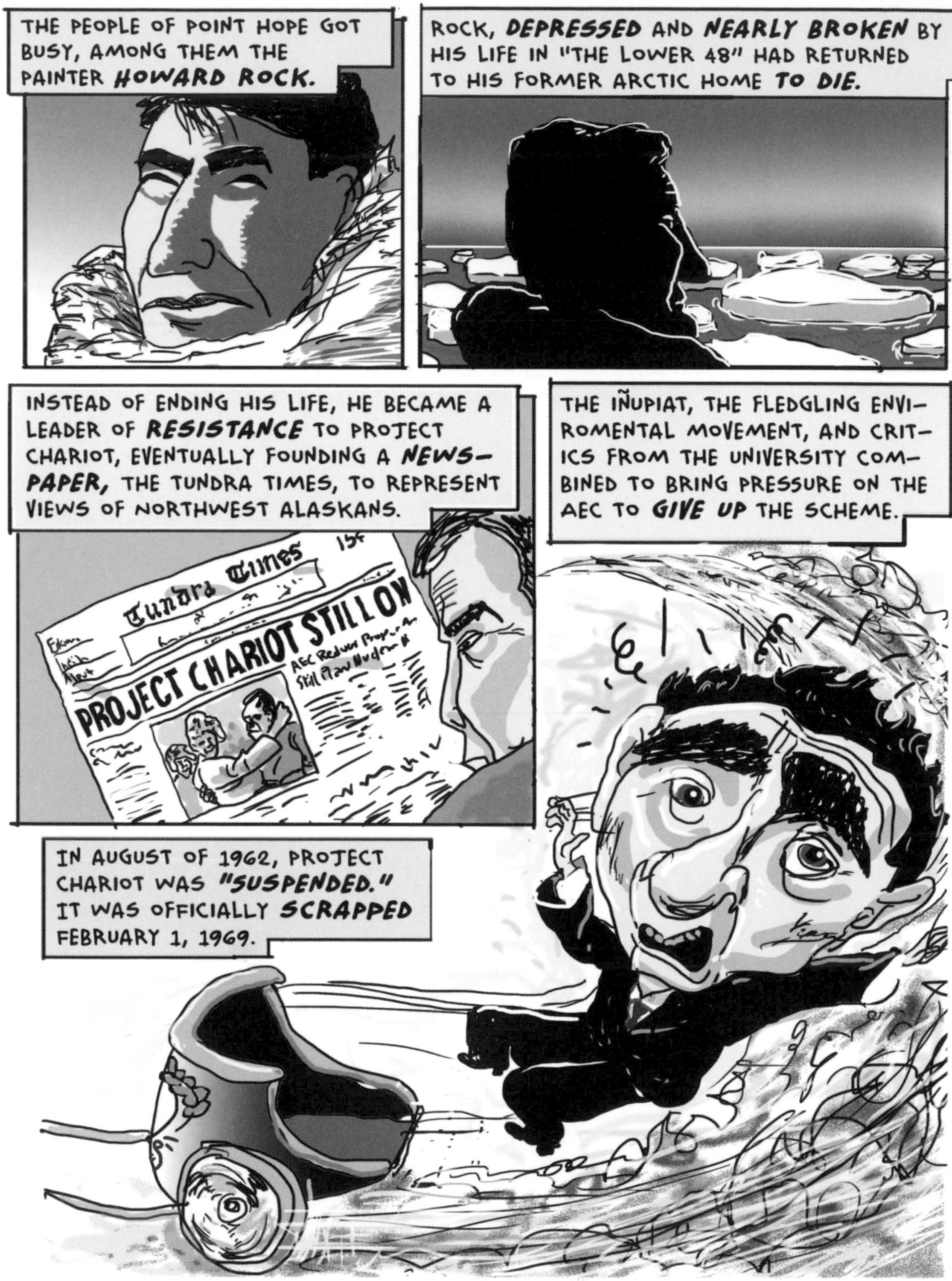
THE PEOPLE OF POINT HOPE GOT BUSY, AMONG THEM THE PAINTER HOWARD ROCK.
ROCK, DEPRESSED AND NEARLY BROKEN BY HIS LIFE IN "THE LOWER 48" HAD RETURNED TO HIS FORMER ARCTIC HOME TO DIE.
INSTEAD OF ENDING HIS LIFE, HE BECAME A LEADER OF RESISTANCE TO PROJECT CHARIOT, EVENTUALLY FOUNDING A NEWSPAPER, THE TUNDRA TIMES, TO REPRESENT VIEWS OF NORTHWEST ALASKANS.
15¢
Tundra Times
PROJECT CHARIOT STILL ON
THE IÑUPIAT, THE FLEDGLING ENVIROMENTAL MOVEMENT, AND CRITICS FROM THE UNIVERSITY COMBINED TO BRING PRESSURE ON THE AEC TO GIVE UP THE SCHEME.
IN AUGUST OF 1962, PROJECT CHARIOT WAS "SUSPENDED." IT WAS OFFICIALLY SCRAPPED FEBRUARY 1, 1969.

THE VICTORY CAME WITH COSTS AND *UNFORESEEN* OUTCOMES. TWO OUT-SPOKEN SCIENTISTS CRITICAL OF THE PROJECT *LOST THEIR JOBS* AT THE *UNIVERSITY.*

YEARS LATER THEIR INTEGRITY WAS RECOGNIZED WITH HONORARY DEGREES.

HALTING THE BLAST WAS AN EARLY *VICTORY* FOR THE ENVIRONMENTAL MOVEMENT AND A *SPUR* TO FURTHER *ECOLOGICAL* ACTION.

NO NUKES

IT WAS AN EMPOWERING ACCOMPLISHMENT FOR *NATIVE POWER,* SETTING THE STAGE FOR THE UPCOMING STRUGGLE IN ALASKA FOR ALASKA NATIVES' *LAND RIGHTS.*

SO THE GOOD GUYS *WON,* AND THE *BAD GUYS* CRAWLED OFF TO LICK THEIR WOUNDS?

NOT EXACTLY. THE AEC QUIETLY IMPORTED *CONTAMINATED MATERIAL* FROM A NUCLEAR TEST IN NEVADA AND BURIED IT IN PITS ON THE CHARIOT SITE TO SEE HOW RADIATION INTERACTED WITH *THE ARCTIC ENVIRONMENT.*

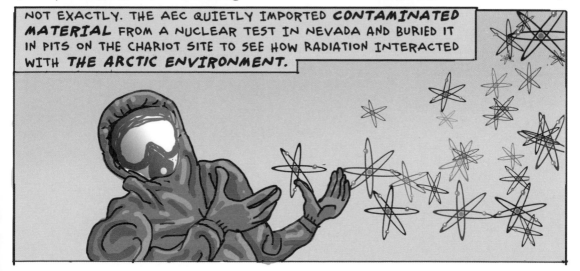

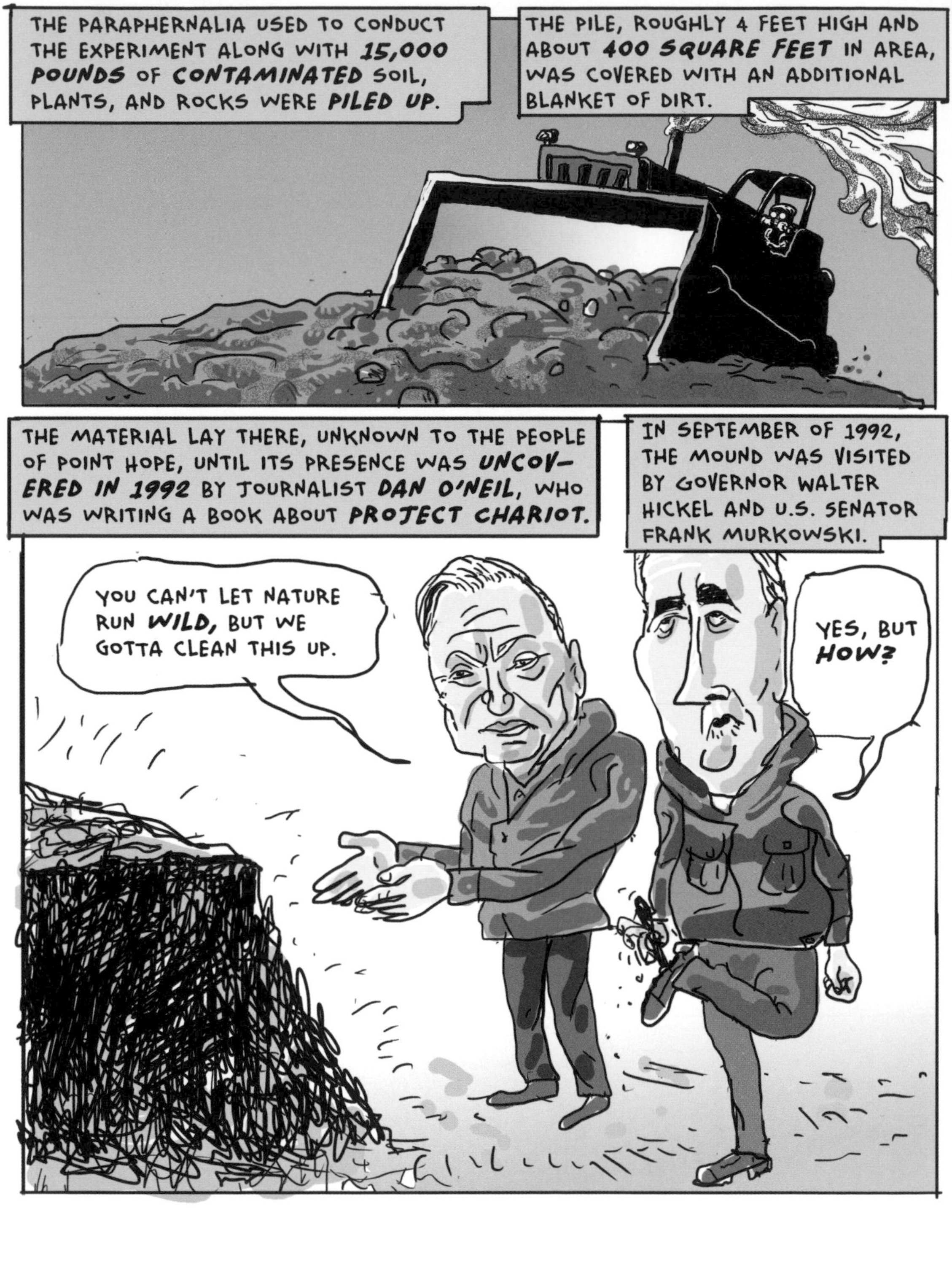
THE PARAPHERNALIA USED TO CONDUCT THE EXPERIMENT ALONG WITH 15,000 POUNDS OF CONTAMINATED SOIL, PLANTS, AND ROCKS WERE PILED UP.
THE PILE, ROUGHLY 4 FEET HIGH AND ABOUT 400 SQUARE FEET IN AREA, WAS COVERED WITH AN ADDITIONAL BLANKET OF DIRT.
THE MATERIAL LAY THERE, UNKNOWN TO THE PEOPLE OF POINT HOPE, UNTIL ITS PRESENCE WAS UNCOVERED IN 1992 BY JOURNALIST DAN O'NEIL, WHO WAS WRITING A BOOK ABOUT PROJECT CHARIOT.
IN SEPTEMBER OF 1992, THE MOUND WAS VISITED BY GOVERNOR WALTER HICKEL AND U.S. SENATOR FRANK MURKOWSKI.
YOU CAN'T LET NATURE RUN WILD, BUT WE GOTTA CLEAN THIS UP.
YES, BUT HOW?

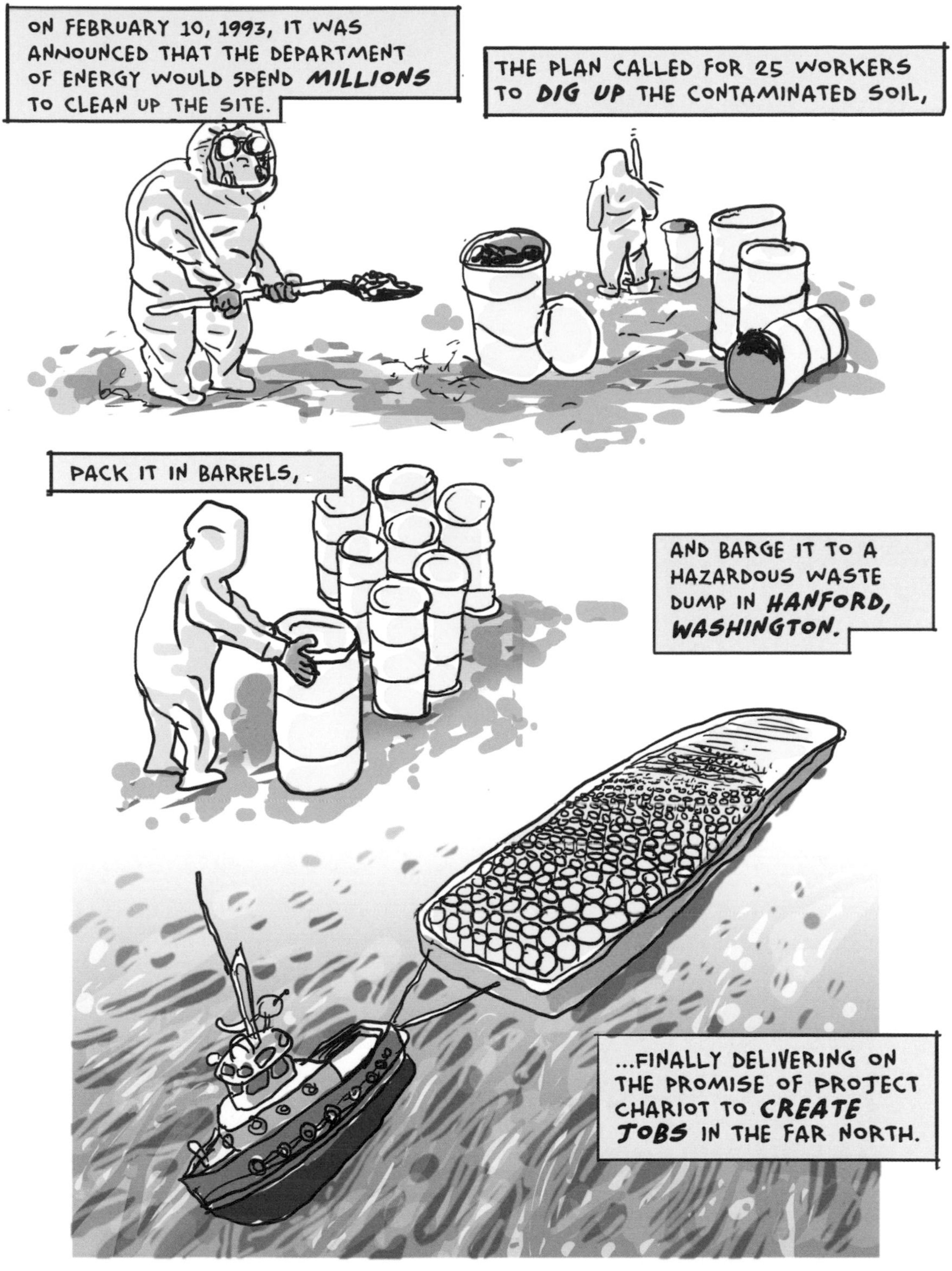
ON FEBRUARY 10, 1993, IT WAS ANNOUNCED THAT THE DEPARTMENT OF ENERGY WOULD SPEND MILLIONS TO CLEAN UP THE SITE.
THE PLAN CALLED FOR 25 WORKERS TO DIG UP THE CONTAMINATED SOIL,
PACK IT IN BARRELS,
AND BARGE IT TO A HAZARDOUS WASTE DUMP IN HANFORD, WASHINGTON.
...FINALLY DELIVERING ON THE PROMISE OF PROJECT CHARIOT TO CREATE JOBS IN THE FAR NORTH.

NUKING ALASKA

3. FRIENDLY FIRE

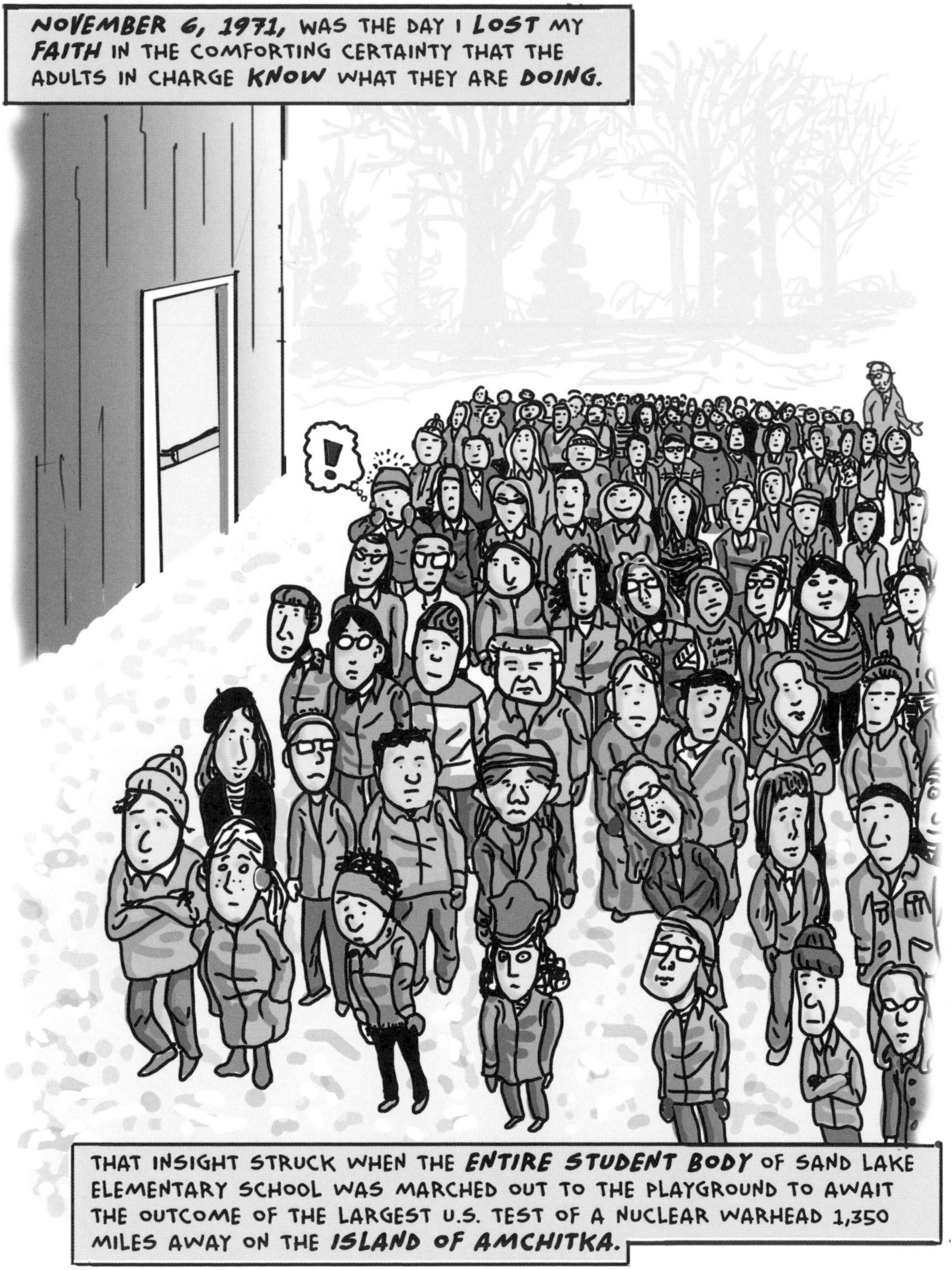
NOVEMBER 6, 1971, WAS THE DAY I LOST MY FAITH IN THE COMFORTING CERTAINTY THAT THE ADULTS IN CHARGE KNOW WHAT THEY ARE DOING.
!
THAT INSIGHT STRUCK WHEN THE ENTIRE STUDENT BODY OF SAND LAKE ELEMENTARY SCHOOL WAS MARCHED OUT TO THE PLAYGROUND TO AWAIT THE OUTCOME OF THE LARGEST U.S. TEST OF A NUCLEAR WARHEAD 1,350 MILES AWAY ON THE ISLAND OF AMCHITKA.

WE STOOD WITH **DREAD** IN THE DIM LIGHT OF EARLY WINTER, HELPLESSLY WAITING FOR THE **MAN-MADE END OF THE WORLD.**

AS OUR TEACHERS MONITORED THEIR WATCHES, IT BECAME PAINFULLY CLEAR THEY DID NOT KNOW WHAT WAS GOING TO HAPPEN ANY MORE THAN OUR **CLASSMATES** DID.

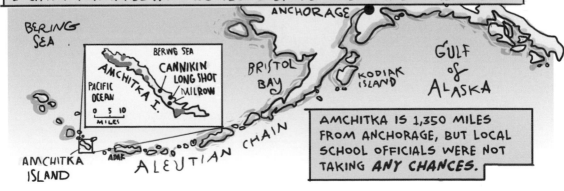

ALASKA'S NUCLEAR LUCK HAD RUN OUT. IT WASN'T ANY FOREIGN THREAT THAT FINALLY CAUGHT UP WITH US: THE ISLAND OF AMCHITKA WAS DESIGNATED THE LOCATION FOR THREE **ATOMIC TESTS** BY THE UNITED STATES GOVERNMENT.

ANCHORAGE

BERING SEA

GULF OF ALASKA

BRISTOL BAY

KODIAK ISLAND

BERING SEA

AMCHITKA I.

CANNIKIN

LONG SHOT

MILROW

PACIFIC OCEAN

0   5   10
MILES

AMCHITKA ISLAND

ADAK

ALEUTIAN CHAIN

AMCHITKA IS 1,350 MILES FROM ANCHORAGE, BUT LOCAL SCHOOL OFFICIALS WERE NOT TAKING **ANY CHANCES.**

CONCERN OVER CAUSING A MASSIVE EARTHQUAKE BY EXPLODING A NUCLEAR WEAPON BENEATH THE TECTONICALLY UNSTABLE VOLCANIC ISLAND WAS ACKNOWLEDGED BY THE DEFENSE DEPARTMENT.

THE SERIES OF TESTS STARTED RELATIVELY SMALL, WITH THE REASSURINGLY NAMED "LONG SHOT," AN 80 KILOTON EXPLOSION.

LONG SHOT
80 KILOTONS, OCTOBER 29, 1965
PURPOSE: TO IMPROVE DETECTION OF SOVIET NUCLEAR TESTS

MILROW
ONE MEGATON, OCTOBER 2, 1969
PURPOSE: TO TEST THE ISLAND'S STABILITY IN PREPARATION FOR CANNIKIN

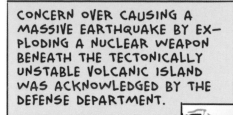

MILES

CANNIKIN
FIVE MEGATONS, NOVEMBER 6, 1971
PURPOSE: APPEASING U.S. RIGHT WING

CANNIKIN-RELATED RUMORS FLEW. BUT WHY WE WERE SAFER OUTDOORS IF THE FABRIC OF THE UNIVERSE *UNRAVELED* WAS *NOT AT ALL* CLEAR.

AND WHY ARE WE OUTSIDE?

IT'S CUZ THE *EXPLOSION* MIGHT CAUSE AN EARTHQUAKE.

AND *TIDAL WAVES!*

BUT WHAT IF BIG CREVICES OPEN IN THE *GROUND?* WOULDN'T IT BE SAFER *INSIDE?*

I'M TOO *YOUNG* TO DIE.

NO YOU'RE NOT.

WHERE IS LANDRY?

HIS PARENTS KEPT HIM HOME TODAY BECAUSE OF THE DANGER, WHATEVER IT IS.

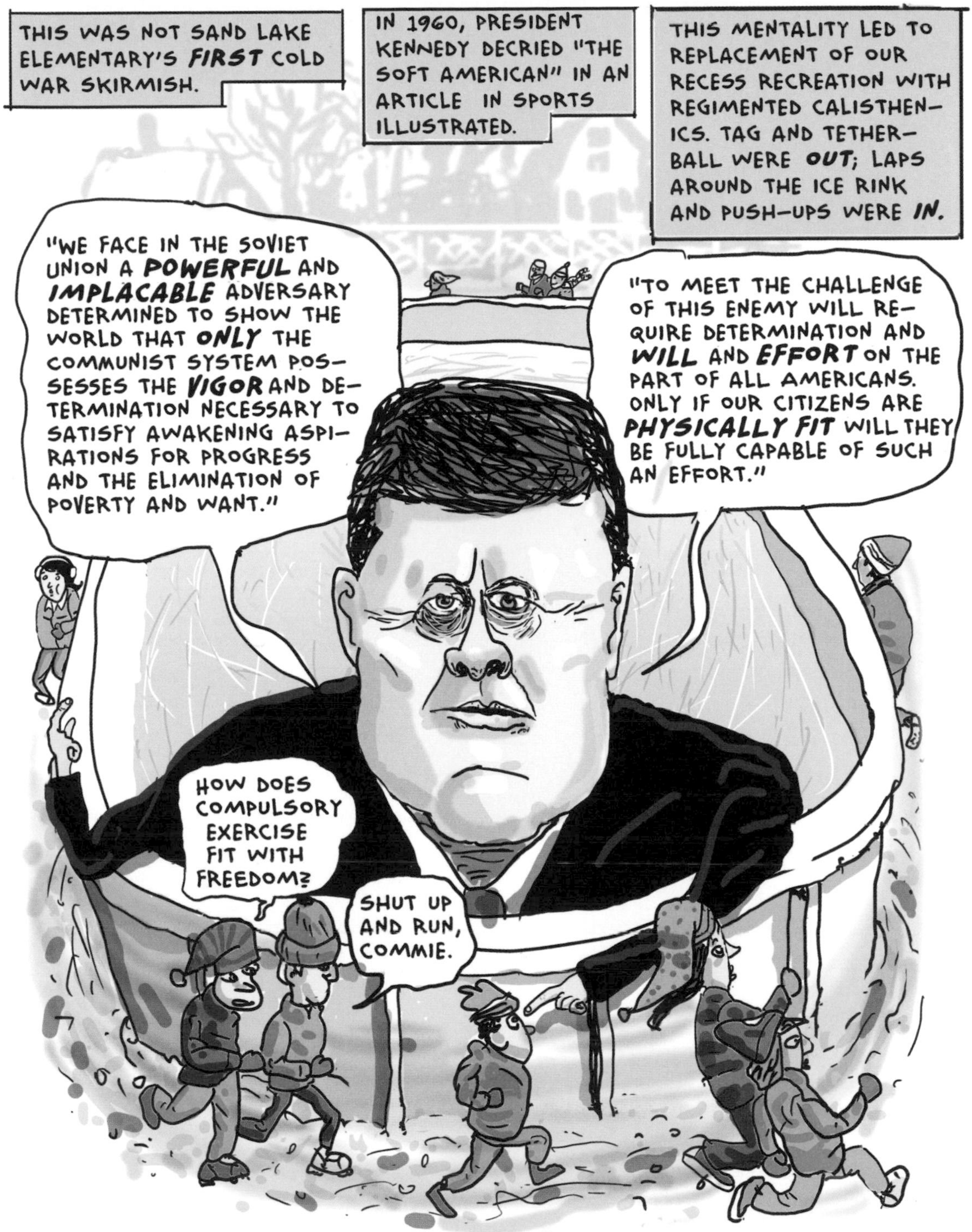
THIS WAS NOT SAND LAKE ELEMENTARY'S FIRST COLD WAR SKIRMISH.
IN 1960, PRESIDENT KENNEDY DECRIED "THE SOFT AMERICAN" IN AN ARTICLE IN SPORTS ILLUSTRATED.
THIS MENTALITY LED TO REPLACEMENT OF OUR RECESS RECREATION WITH REGIMENTED CALISTHENICS. TAG AND TETHERBALL WERE OUT; LAPS AROUND THE ICE RINK AND PUSH-UPS WERE IN.
"WE FACE IN THE SOVIET UNION A POWERFUL AND IMPLACABLE ADVERSARY DETERMINED TO SHOW THE WORLD THAT ONLY THE COMMUNIST SYSTEM POSSESSES THE VIGOR AND DETERMINATION NECESSARY TO SATISFY AWAKENING ASPIRATIONS FOR PROGRESS AND THE ELIMINATION OF POVERTY AND WANT."
"TO MEET THE CHALLENGE OF THIS ENEMY WILL REQUIRE DETERMINATION AND WILL AND EFFORT ON THE PART OF ALL AMERICANS. ONLY IF OUR CITIZENS ARE PHYSICALLY FIT WILL THEY BE FULLY CAPABLE OF SUCH AN EFFORT."
HOW DOES COMPULSORY EXERCISE FIT WITH FREEDOM?
SHUT UP AND RUN, COMMIE.

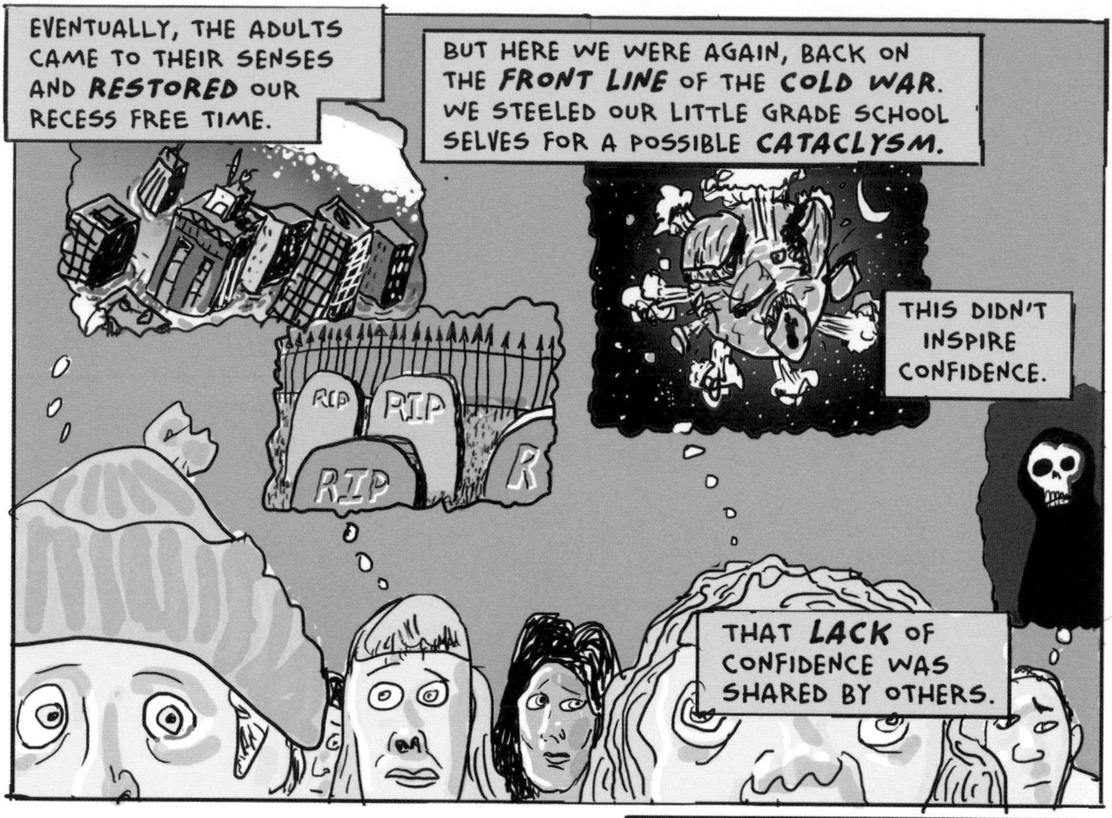
EVENTUALLY, THE ADULTS CAME TO THEIR SENSES AND RESTORED OUR RECESS FREE TIME.
BUT HERE WE WERE AGAIN, BACK ON THE FRONT LINE OF THE COLD WAR. WE STEELED OUR LITTLE GRADE SCHOOL SELVES FOR A POSSIBLE CATACLYSM.
RIP
RIP
RIP
R
THIS DIDN'T INSPIRE CONFIDENCE.
THAT LACK OF CONFIDENCE WAS SHARED BY OTHERS.

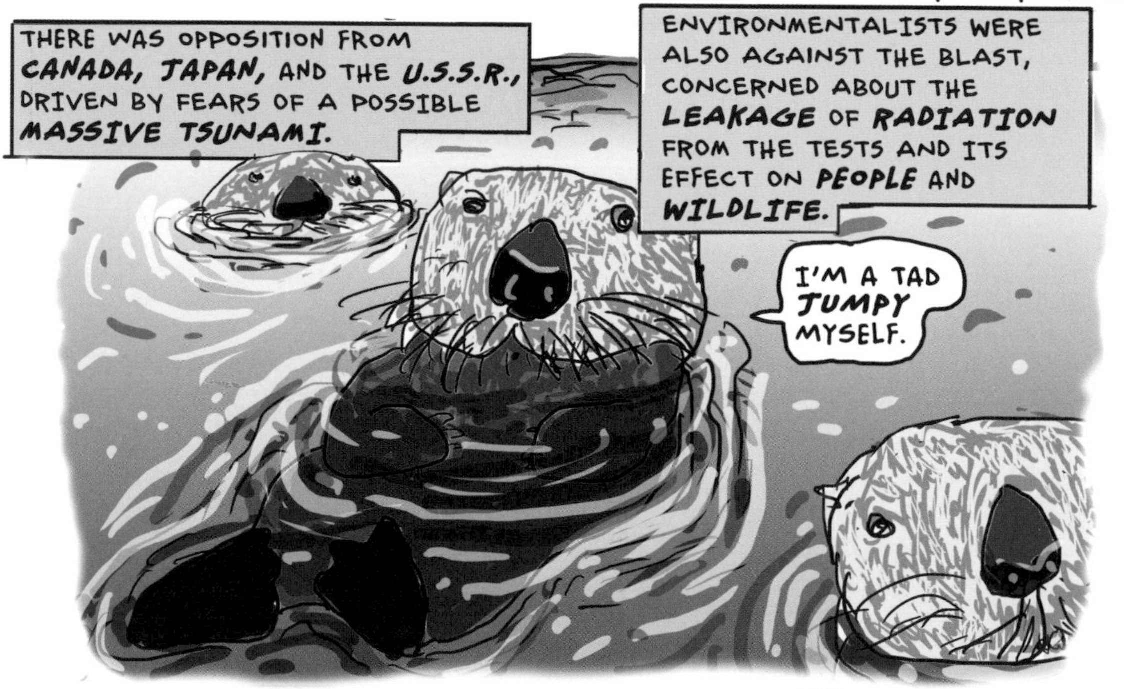
THERE WAS OPPOSITION FROM CANADA, JAPAN, AND THE U.S.S.R., DRIVEN BY FEARS OF A POSSIBLE MASSIVE TSUNAMI.
ENVIRONMENTALISTS WERE ALSO AGAINST THE BLAST, CONCERNED ABOUT THE LEAKAGE OF RADIATION FROM THE TESTS AND ITS EFFECT ON PEOPLE AND WILDLIFE.
I'M A TAD JUMPY MYSELF.

SOME WOULD CALL AMCHITKA ***INHOSPITABLE*** WITH ITS CONSTANT ***RAIN*** AND ***WIND.*** FOR WILDLIFE, IT IS A ***HAVEN.***

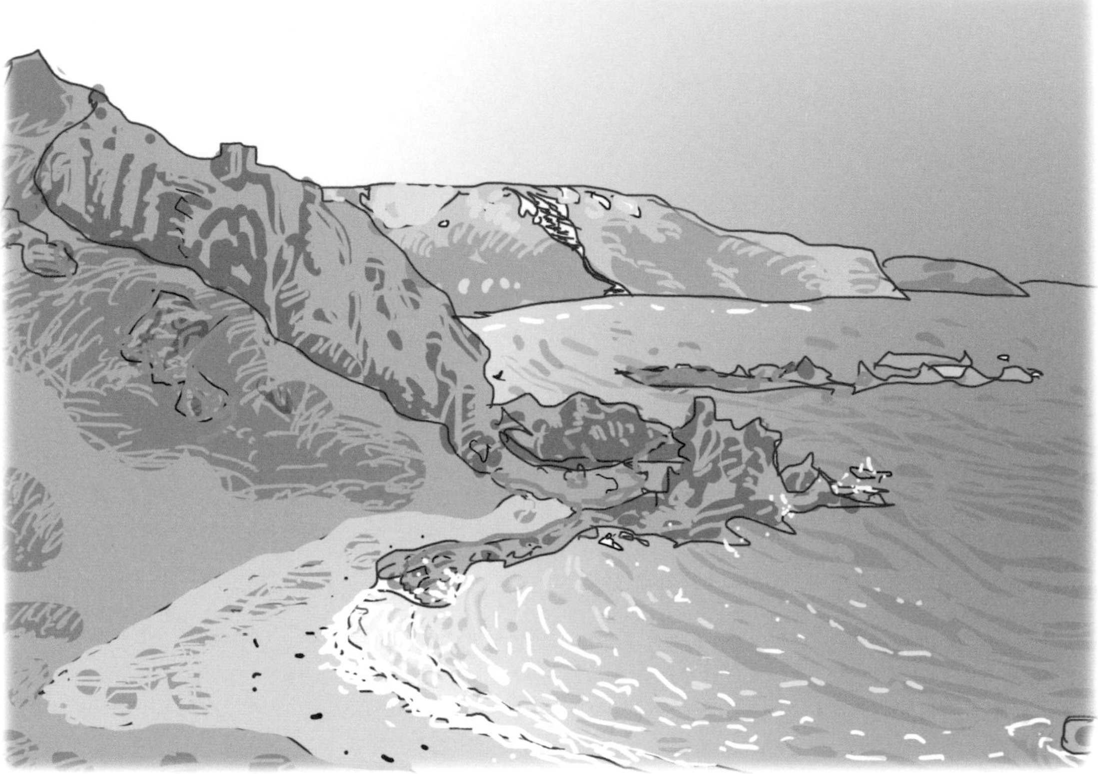

THE ISLAND IS HOME TO STELLER SEA LIONS, SEA OTTERS, AND NEARLY ***100 SPECIES*** OF ***BIRDS,*** INCLUDING ***BALD EAGLES*** AND ***TUFTED PUFFINS.***

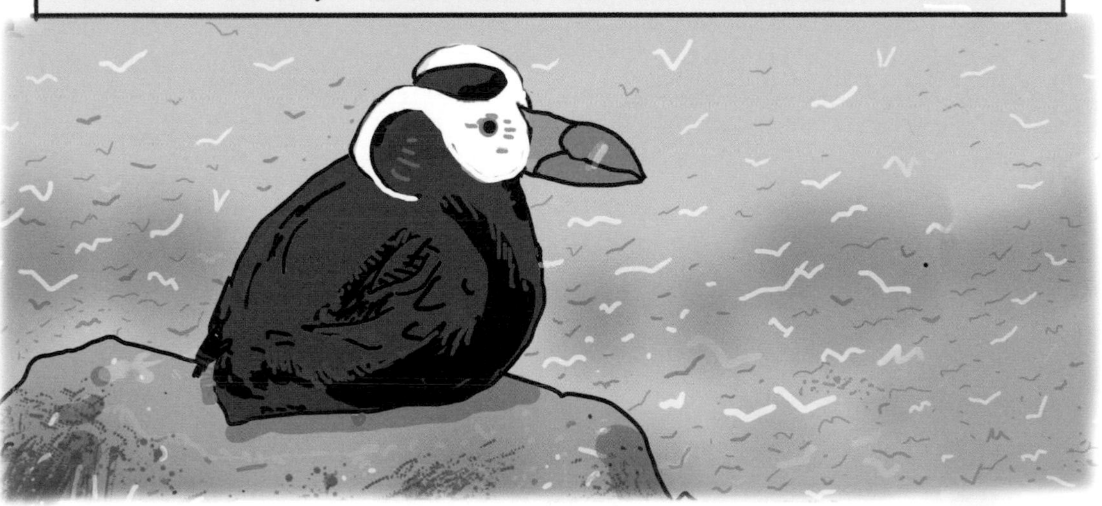

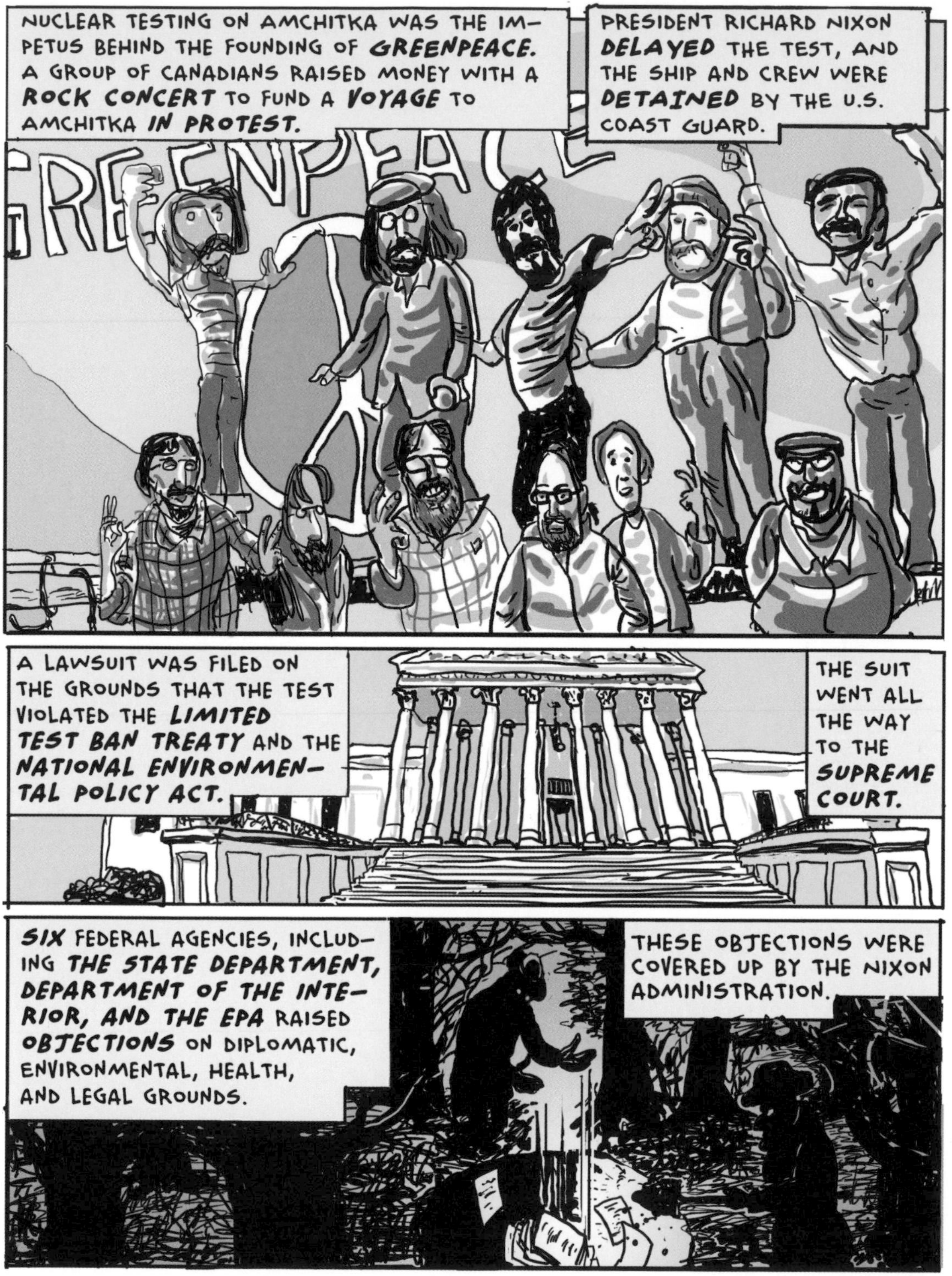
NUCLEAR TESTING ON AMCHITKA WAS THE IMPETUS BEHIND THE FOUNDING OF GREENPEACE. A GROUP OF CANADIANS RAISED MONEY WITH A ROCK CONCERT TO FUND A VOYAGE TO AMCHITKA IN PROTEST.
PRESIDENT RICHARD NIXON DELAYED THE TEST, AND THE SHIP AND CREW WERE DETAINED BY THE U.S. COAST GUARD.
GREENPEACE
A LAWSUIT WAS FILED ON THE GROUNDS THAT THE TEST VIOLATED THE LIMITED TEST BAN TREATY AND THE NATIONAL ENVIRONMENTAL POLICY ACT.
THE SUIT WENT ALL THE WAY TO THE SUPREME COURT.
SIX FEDERAL AGENCIES, INCLUDING THE STATE DEPARTMENT, DEPARTMENT OF THE INTERIOR, AND THE EPA RAISED OBJECTIONS ON DIPLOMATIC, ENVIRONMENTAL, HEALTH, AND LEGAL GROUNDS.
THESE OBJECTIONS WERE COVERED UP BY THE NIXON ADMINISTRATION.

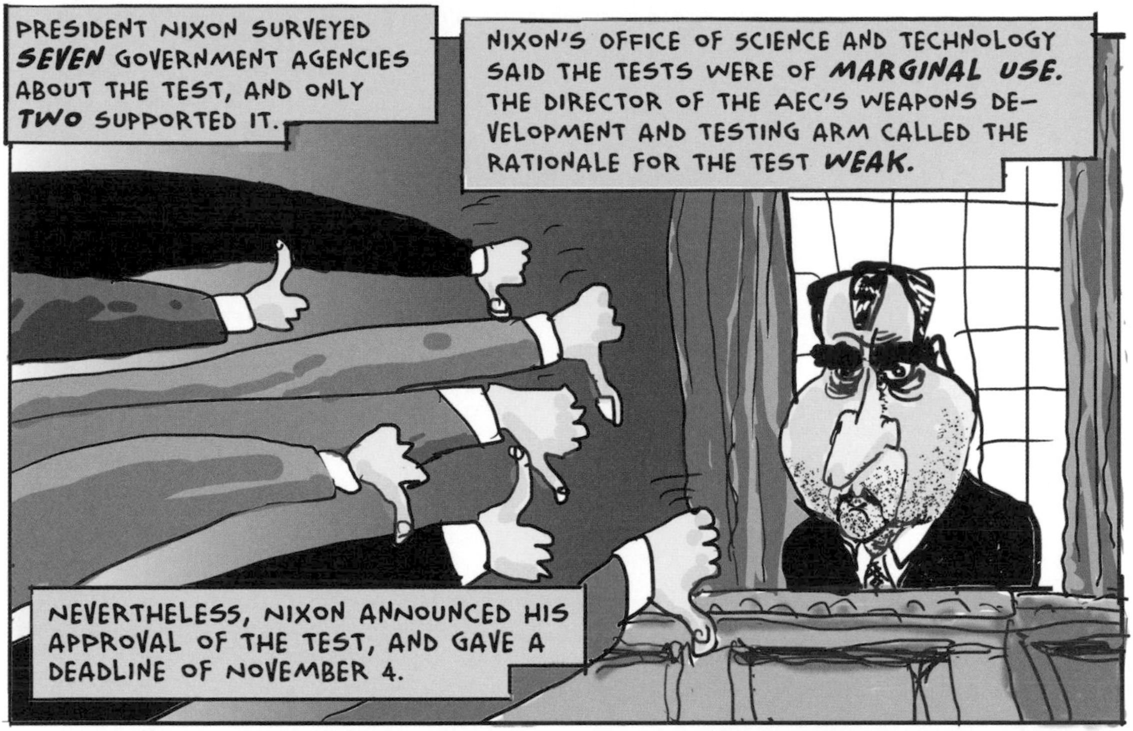
PRESIDENT NIXON SURVEYED SEVEN GOVERNMENT AGENCIES ABOUT THE TEST, AND ONLY TWO SUPPORTED IT.
NIXON'S OFFICE OF SCIENCE AND TECHNOLOGY SAID THE TESTS WERE OF MARGINAL USE. THE DIRECTOR OF THE AEC'S WEAPONS DEVELOPMENT AND TESTING ARM CALLED THE RATIONALE FOR THE TEST WEAK.
NEVERTHELESS, NIXON ANNOUNCED HIS APPROVAL OF THE TEST, AND GAVE A DEADLINE OF NOVEMBER 4.

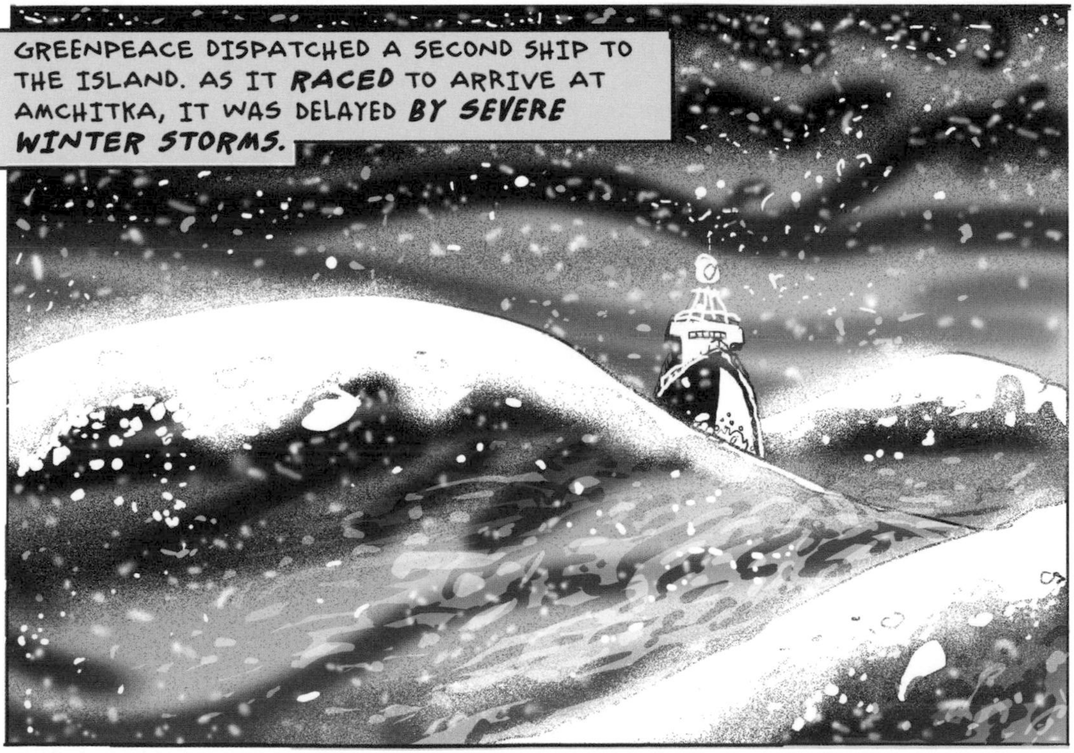
GREENPEACE DISPATCHED A SECOND SHIP TO THE ISLAND. AS IT RACED TO ARRIVE AT AMCHITKA, IT WAS DELAYED BY SEVERE WINTER STORMS.

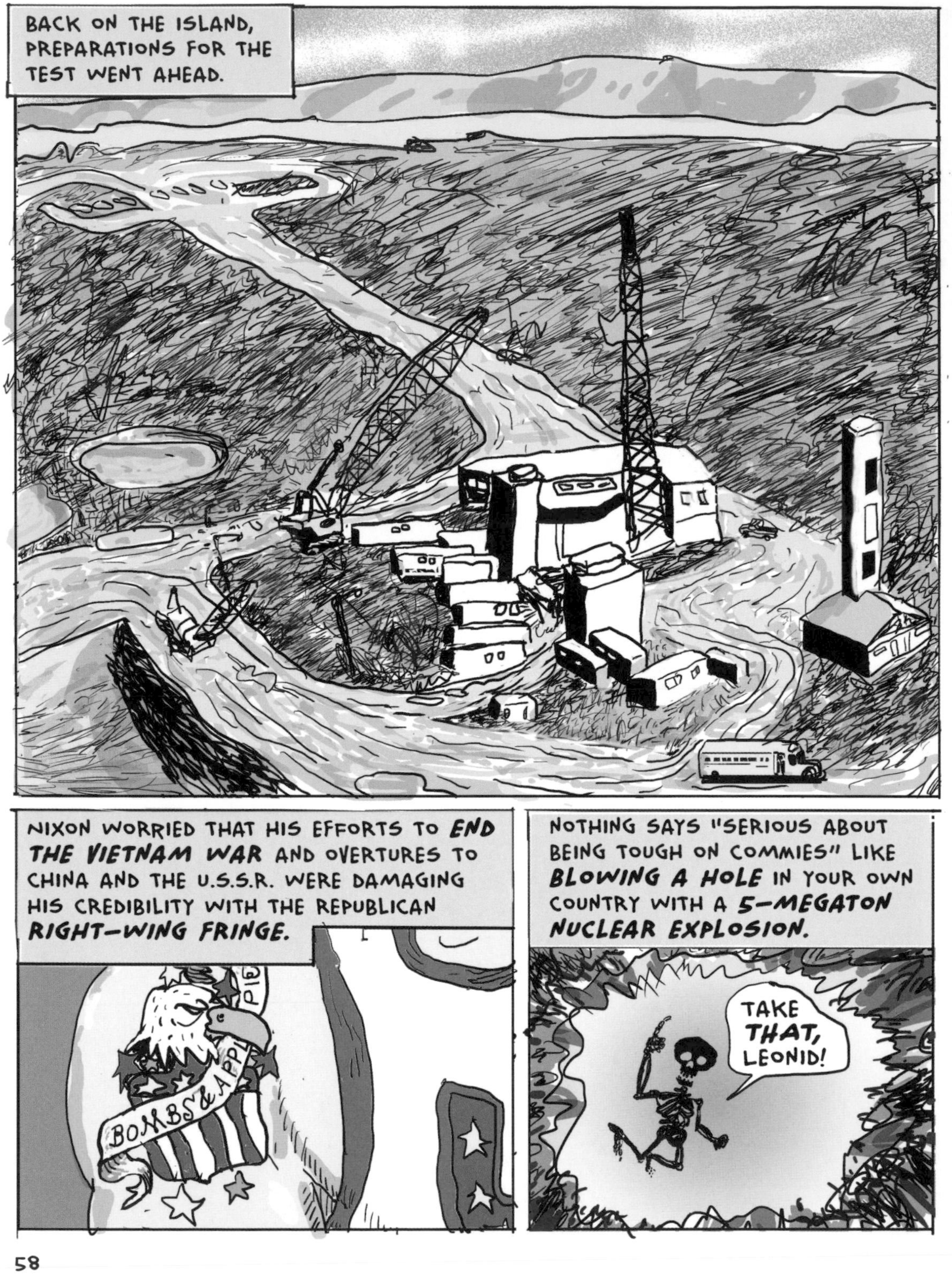
BACK ON THE ISLAND, PREPARATIONS FOR THE TEST WENT AHEAD.
NIXON WORRIED THAT HIS EFFORTS TO **END THE VIETNAM WAR** AND OVERTURES TO CHINA AND THE U.S.S.R. WERE DAMAGING HIS CREDIBILITY WITH THE REPUBLICAN **RIGHT-WING FRINGE.**
NOTHING SAYS "SERIOUS ABOUT BEING TOUGH ON COMMIES" LIKE **BLOWING A HOLE** IN YOUR OWN COUNTRY WITH A **5-MEGATON NUCLEAR EXPLOSION.**
TAKE **THAT,** LEONID!

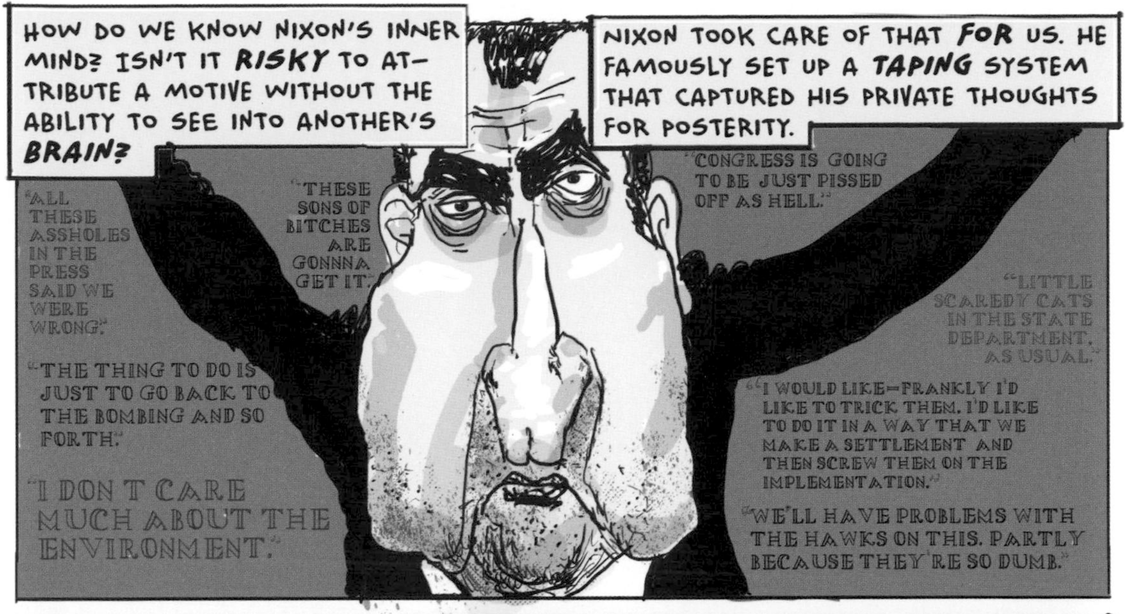
HOW DO WE KNOW NIXON'S INNER MIND? ISN'T IT *RISKY* TO ATTRIBUTE A MOTIVE WITHOUT THE ABILITY TO SEE INTO ANOTHER'S *BRAIN?*
NIXON TOOK CARE OF THAT *FOR* US. HE FAMOUSLY SET UP A *TAPING* SYSTEM THAT CAPTURED HIS PRIVATE THOUGHTS FOR POSTERITY.
"ALL THESE ASSHOLES IN THE PRESS SAID WE WERE WRONG."
"THESE SONS OF BITCHES ARE GONNNA GET IT."
"CONGRESS IS GOING TO BE JUST PISSED OFF AS HELL."
"LITTLE SCAREDY CATS IN THE STATE DEPARTMENT, AS USUAL."
"THE THING TO DO IS JUST TO GO BACK TO THE BOMBING AND SO FORTH."
"I WOULD LIKE—FRANKLY I'D LIKE TO TRICK THEM. I'D LIKE TO DO IT IN A WAY THAT WE MAKE A SETTLEMENT AND THEN SCREW THEM ON THE IMPLEMENTATION."
"I DON T CARE MUCH ABOUT THE ENVIRONMENT."
"WE'LL HAVE PROBLEMS WITH THE HAWKS ON THIS. PARTLY BECAUSE THEY'RE SO DUMB."

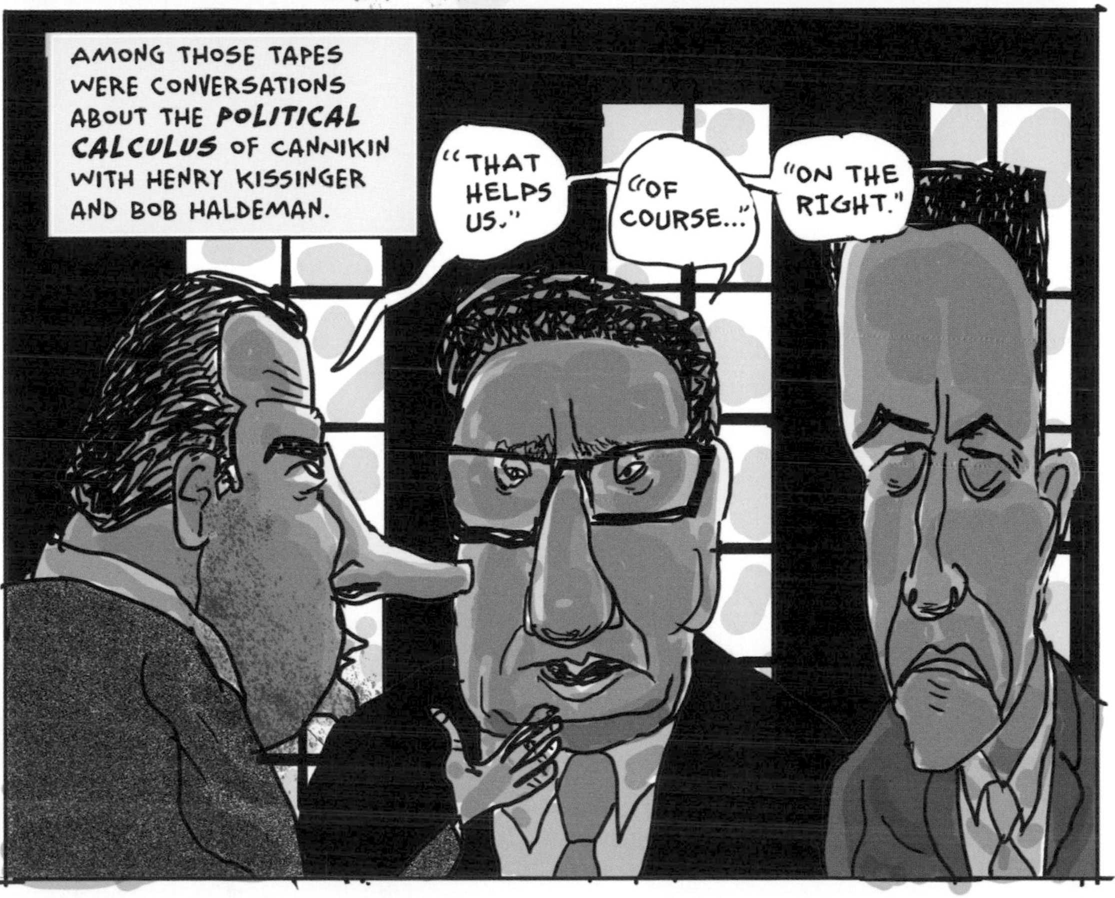
AMONG THOSE TAPES WERE CONVERSATIONS ABOUT THE *POLITICAL CALCULUS* OF CANNIKIN WITH HENRY KISSINGER AND BOB HALDEMAN.
"THAT HELPS US."
"OF COURSE..."
"ON THE RIGHT."

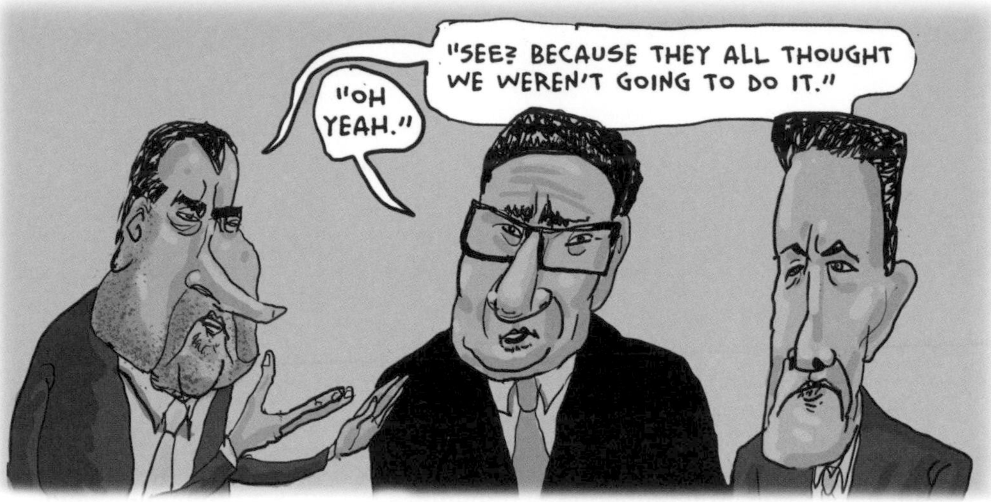
"OH YEAH."
"SEE? BECAUSE THEY ALL THOUGHT WE WEREN'T GOING TO DO IT."

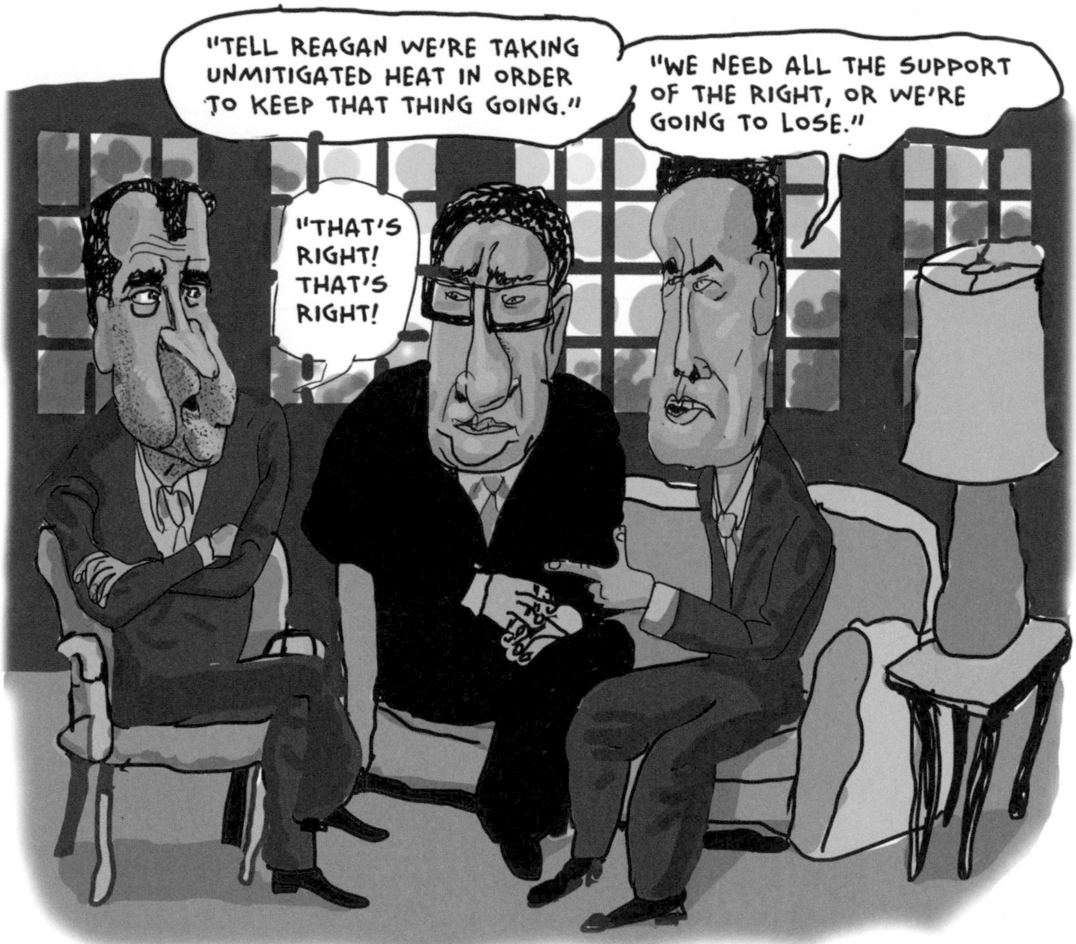
"TELL REAGAN WE'RE TAKING UNMITIGATED HEAT IN ORDER TO KEEP THAT THING GOING."
"THAT'S RIGHT! THAT'S RIGHT!
"WE NEED ALL THE SUPPORT OF THE RIGHT, OR WE'RE GOING TO LOSE."

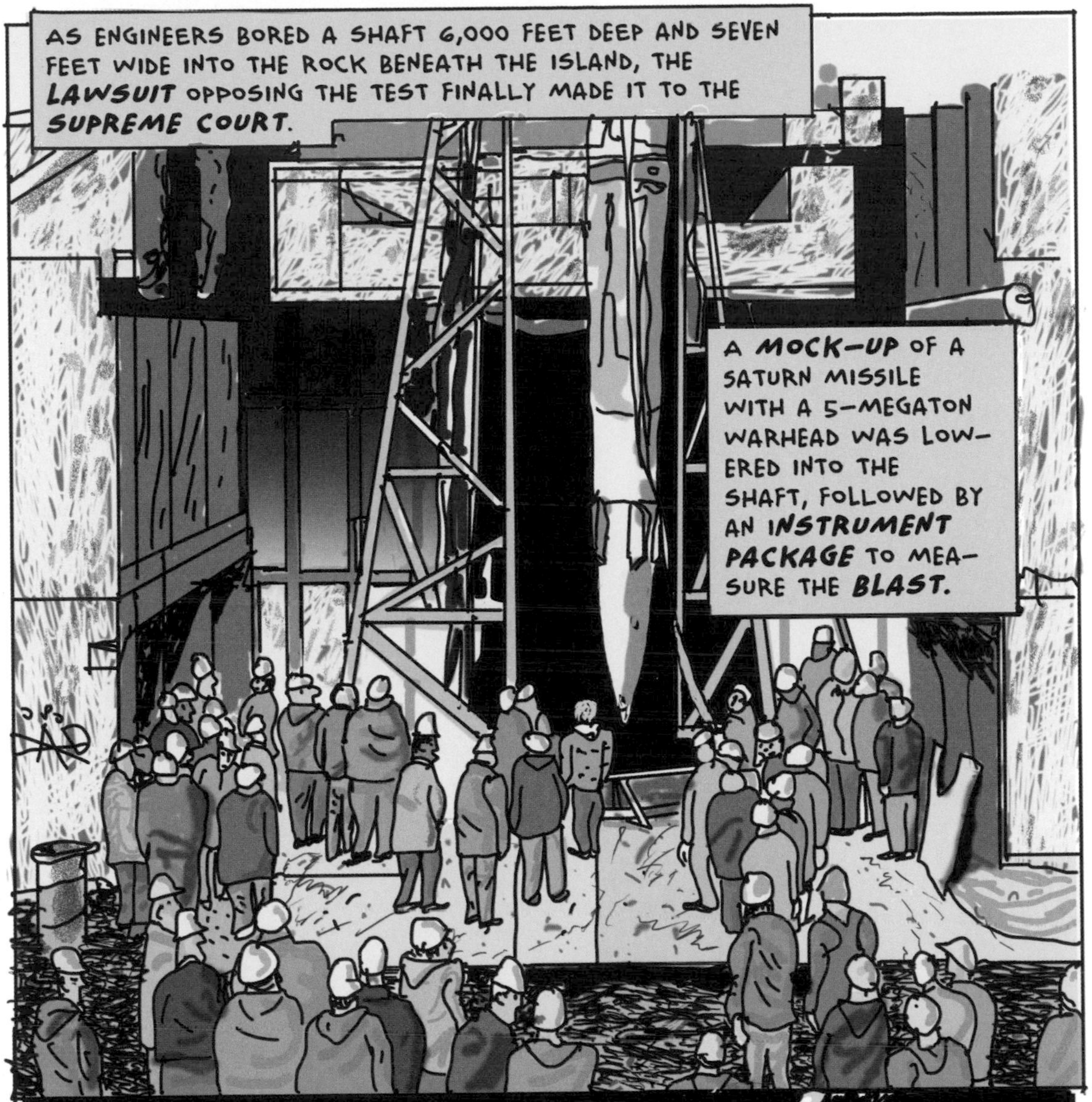
AS ENGINEERS BORED A SHAFT 6,000 FEET DEEP AND SEVEN FEET WIDE INTO THE ROCK BENEATH THE ISLAND, THE LAWSUIT OPPOSING THE TEST FINALLY MADE IT TO THE SUPREME COURT.
A MOCK-UP OF A SATURN MISSILE WITH A 5-MEGATON WARHEAD WAS LOWERED INTO THE SHAFT, FOLLOWED BY AN INSTRUMENT PACKAGE TO MEASURE THE BLAST.

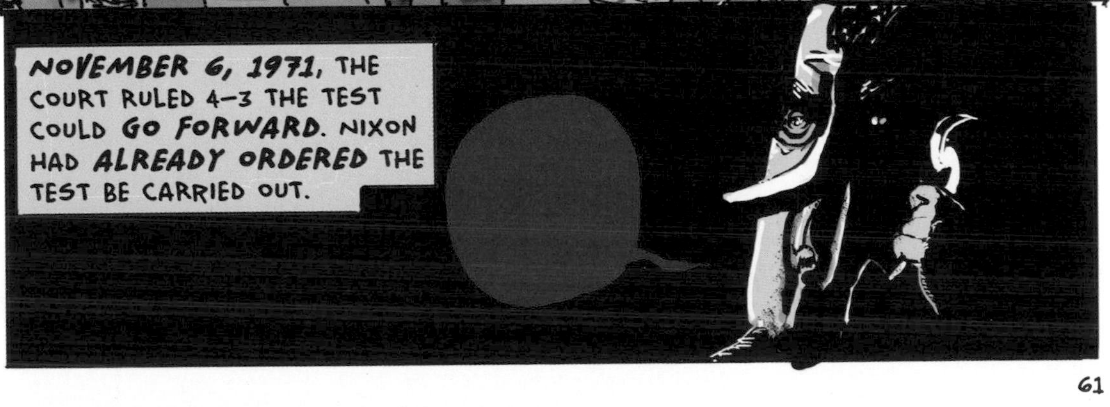
NOVEMBER 6, 1971, THE COURT RULED 4-3 THE TEST COULD GO FORWARD. NIXON HAD ALREADY ORDERED THE TEST BE CARRIED OUT.

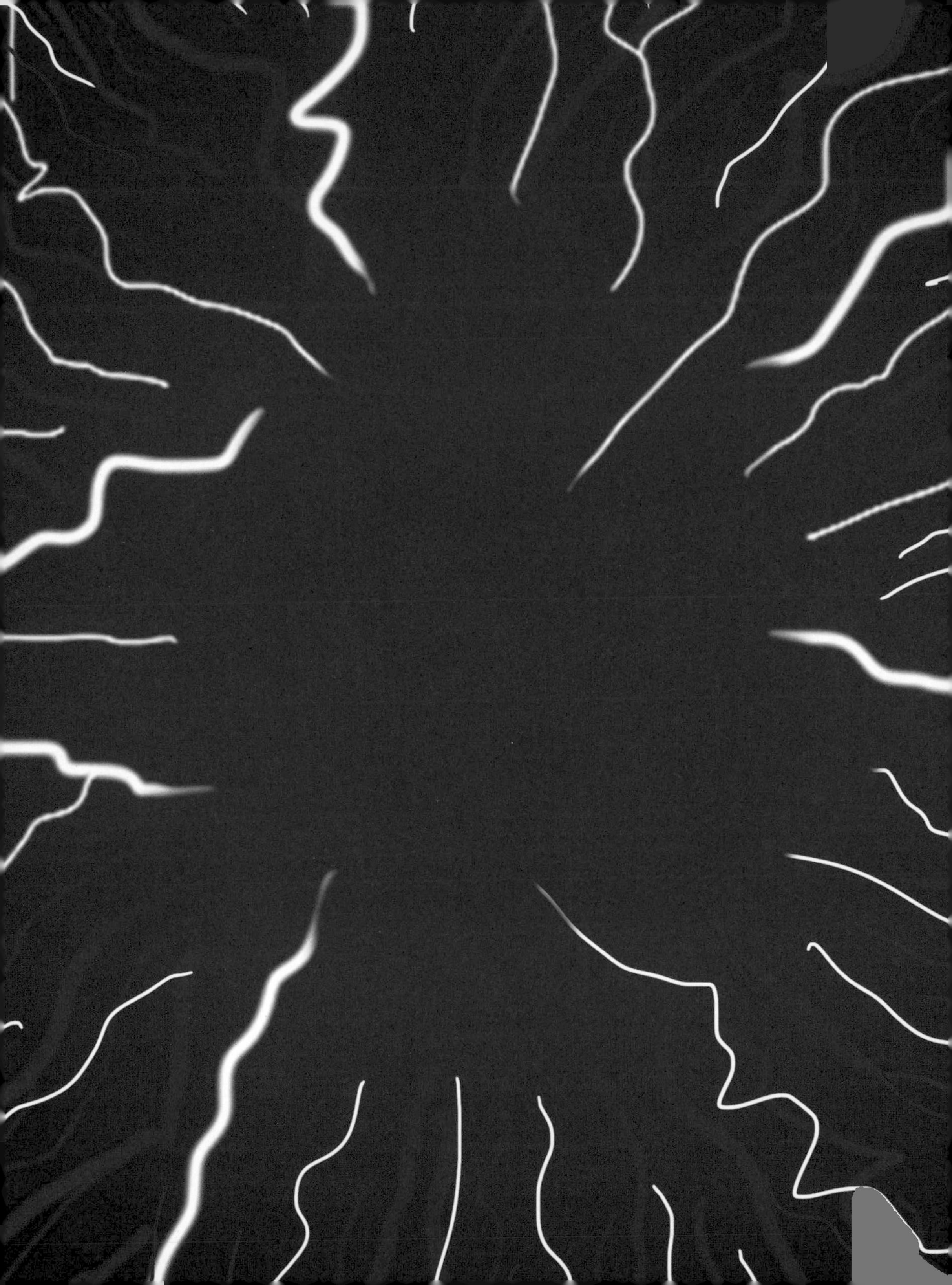

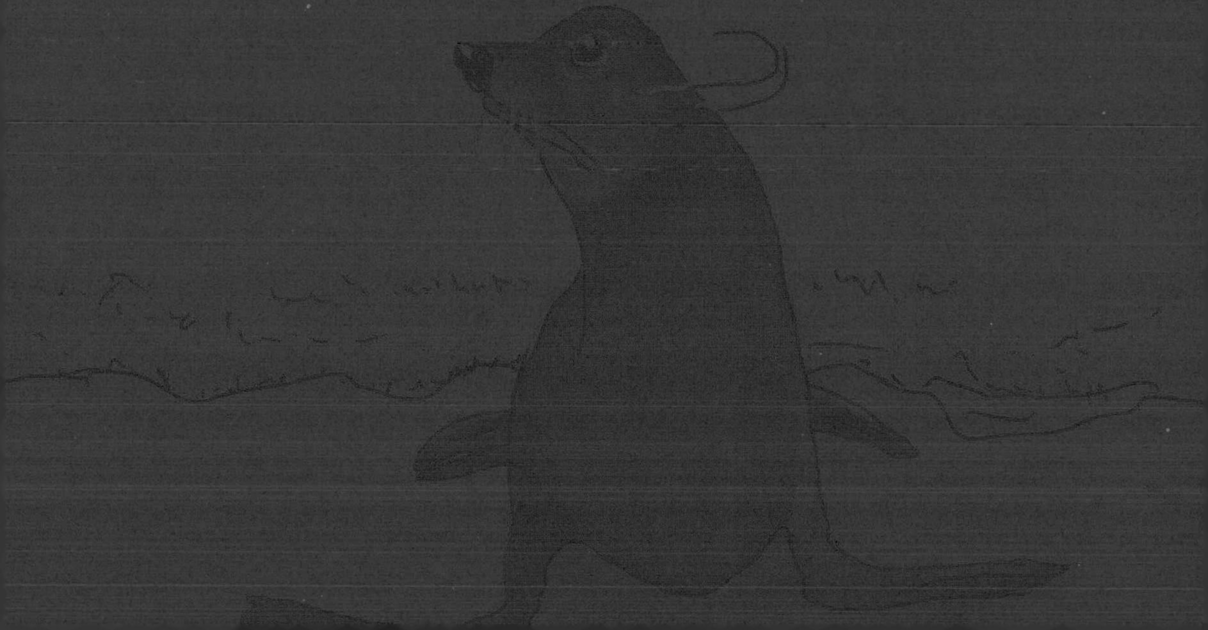

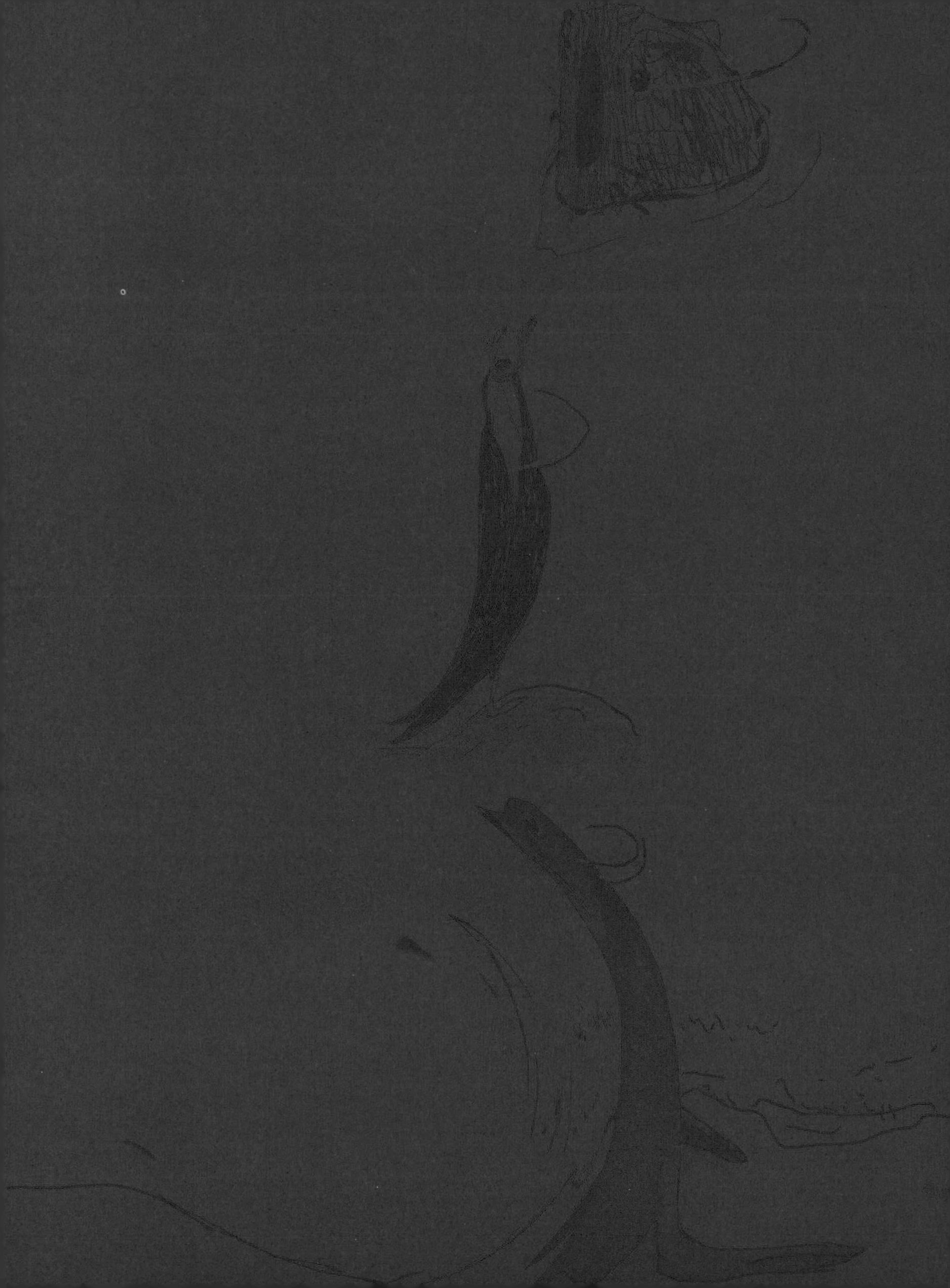

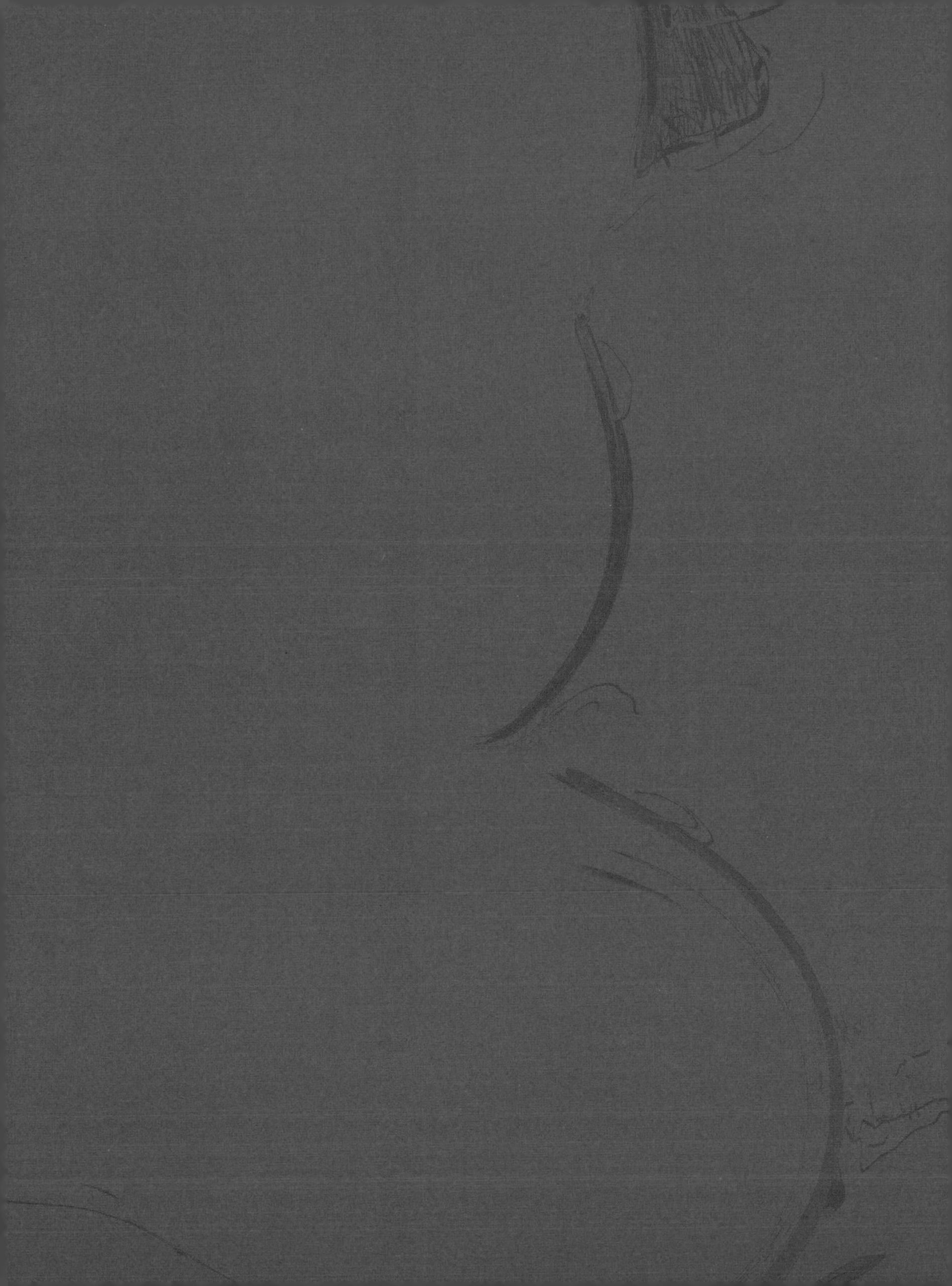

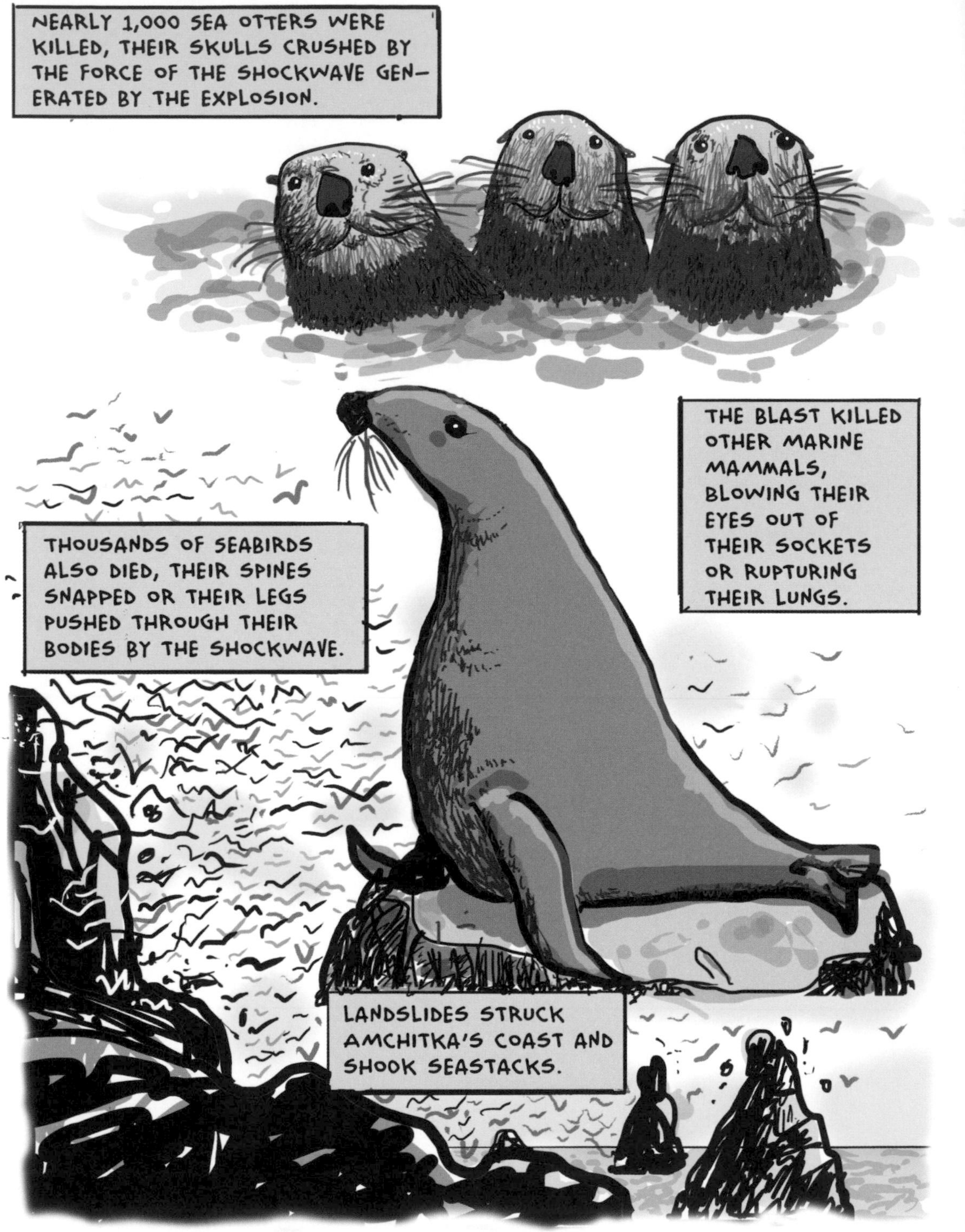
NEARLY 1,000 SEA OTTERS WERE KILLED, THEIR SKULLS CRUSHED BY THE FORCE OF THE SHOCKWAVE GENERATED BY THE EXPLOSION.
THOUSANDS OF SEABIRDS ALSO DIED, THEIR SPINES SNAPPED OR THEIR LEGS PUSHED THROUGH THEIR BODIES BY THE SHOCKWAVE.
THE BLAST KILLED OTHER MARINE MAMMALS, BLOWING THEIR EYES OUT OF THEIR SOCKETS OR RUPTURING THEIR LUNGS.
LANDSLIDES STRUCK AMCHITKA'S COAST AND SHOOK SEASTACKS.

A CLASSIFIED FILM MADE AT THE TIME OF THE TEST **HAILED IT** AS A **GREAT SUCCESS**, AMONG THE FACTORS CITED WERE THE CONTAINMENT OF RADIATION. THE **LACK OF DAMAGE** TO THE ISLAND'S ENVIRONMENT, AND **MINIMAL HARM** TO AREA WILDLIFE.

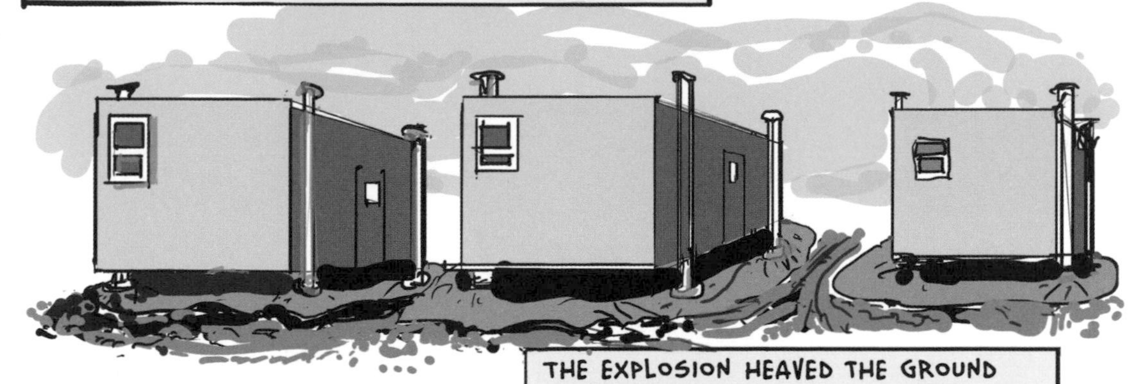

THE EXPLOSION HEAVED THE GROUND **25 FEET** IN THE AIR IN THE VICINITY OF THE BLAST CHIMNEY.

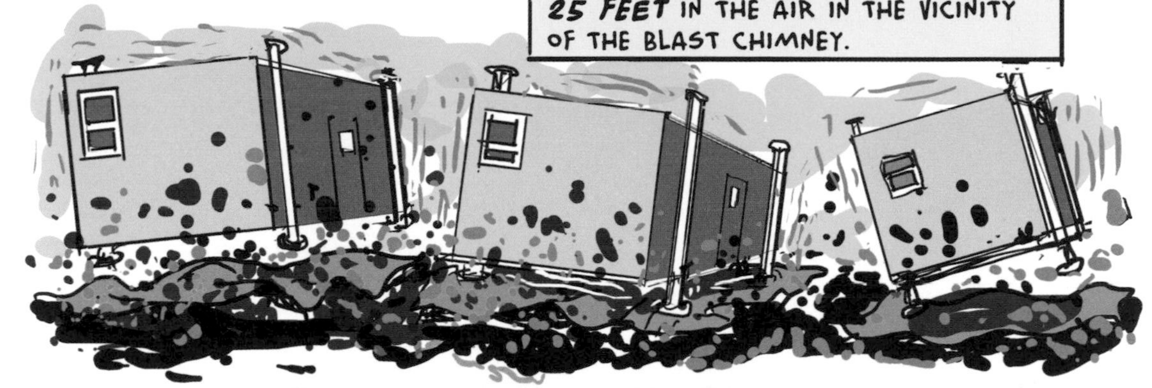

TRAILERS CONTAINING INSTRUMENTS TO MEASURE THE EFFECTS OF THE TEST WERE **TOSSED** LIKE **DRY LEAVES.**

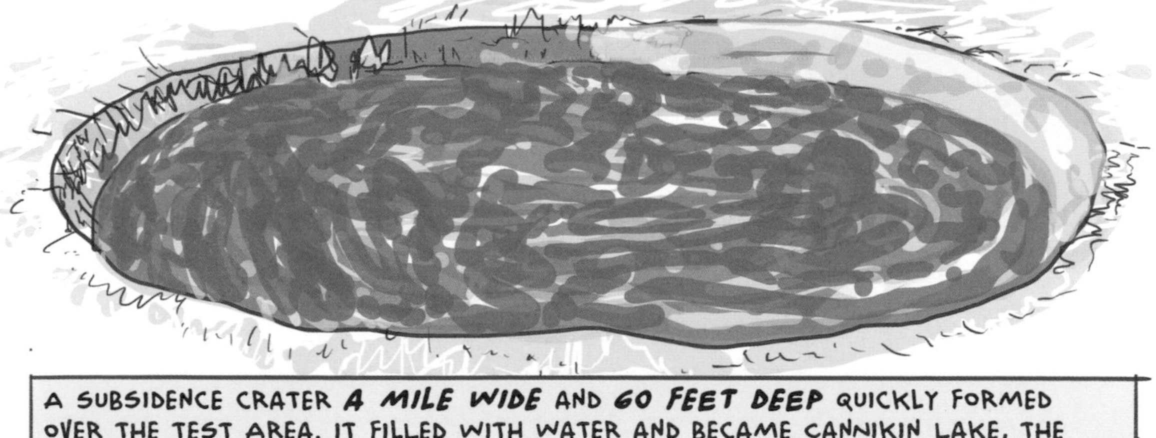

A SUBSIDENCE CRATER **A MILE WIDE** AND **60 FEET DEEP** QUICKLY FORMED OVER THE TEST AREA. IT FILLED WITH WATER AND BECAME CANNIKIN LAKE, THE **LARGEST LAKE** ON THE ISLAND.

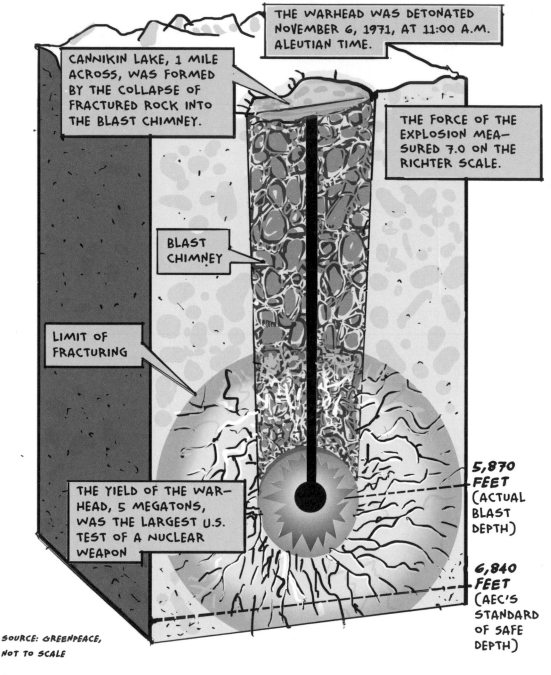

THE MISSILE MOCK-UP, ARMED WITH ITS LIVE WARHEAD, DESCENDED 5,870 FEET INTO THE SHAFT, *1,000 FEET LESS* THAN THE *AEC'S STANDARD* FOR CONTAINMENT OF A BLAST OF THIS MAGNITUDE. THE SCIENTISTS RETREATED TO THE OTHER END OF THE ISLAND.

THE WARHEAD WAS DETONATED NOVEMBER 6, 1971, AT 11:00 A.M. ALEUTIAN TIME.

CANNIKIN LAKE, 1 MILE ACROSS, WAS FORMED BY THE COLLAPSE OF FRACTURED ROCK INTO THE BLAST CHIMNEY.

THE FORCE OF THE EXPLOSION MEASURED 7.0 ON THE RICHTER SCALE.

BLAST CHIMNEY

LIMIT OF FRACTURING

THE YIELD OF THE WARHEAD, 5 MEGATONS, WAS THE LARGEST U.S. TEST OF A NUCLEAR WEAPON

5,870 FEET (ACTUAL BLAST DEPTH)

6,840 FEET (AEC'S STANDARD OF SAFE DEPTH)

SOURCE: GREENPEACE, NOT TO SCALE

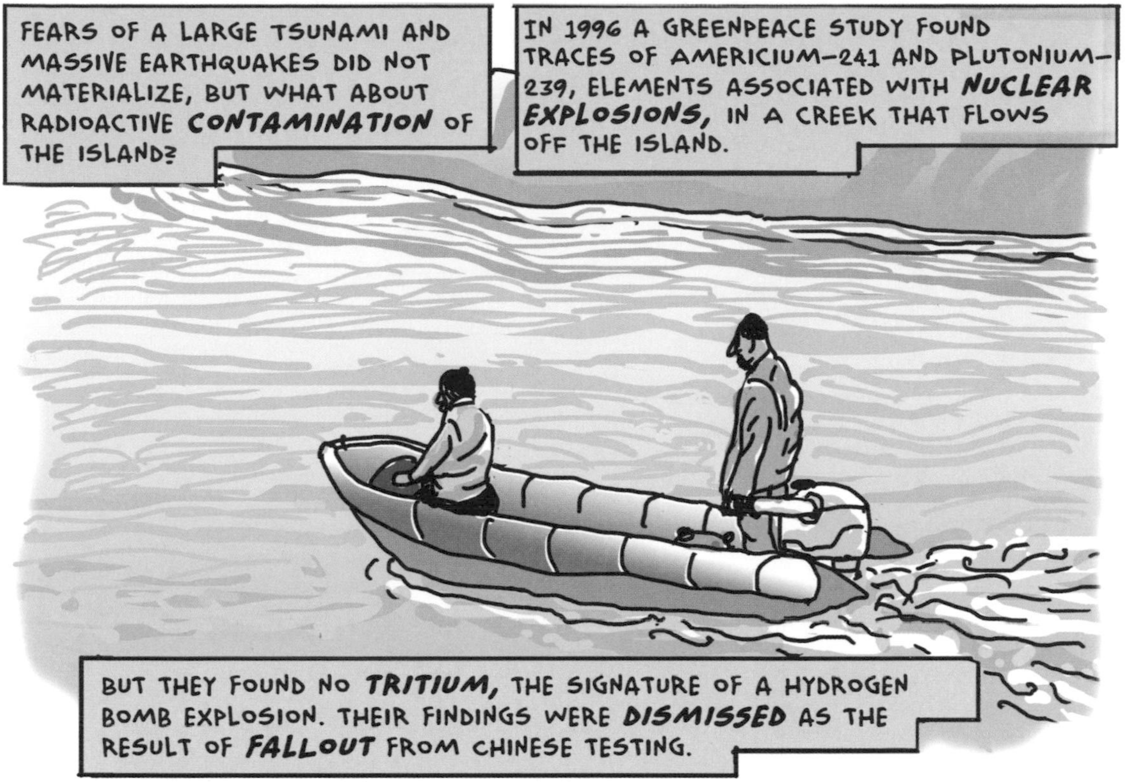
FEARS OF A LARGE TSUNAMI AND MASSIVE EARTHQUAKES DID NOT MATERIALIZE, BUT WHAT ABOUT RADIOACTIVE **CONTAMINATION** OF THE ISLAND?
IN 1996 A GREENPEACE STUDY FOUND TRACES OF AMERICIUM-241 AND PLUTONIUM-239, ELEMENTS ASSOCIATED WITH ***NUCLEAR EXPLOSIONS,*** IN A CREEK THAT FLOWS OFF THE ISLAND.
BUT THEY FOUND NO ***TRITIUM,*** THE SIGNATURE OF A HYDROGEN BOMB EXPLOSION. THEIR FINDINGS WERE ***DISMISSED*** AS THE RESULT OF ***FALLOUT*** FROM CHINESE TESTING.

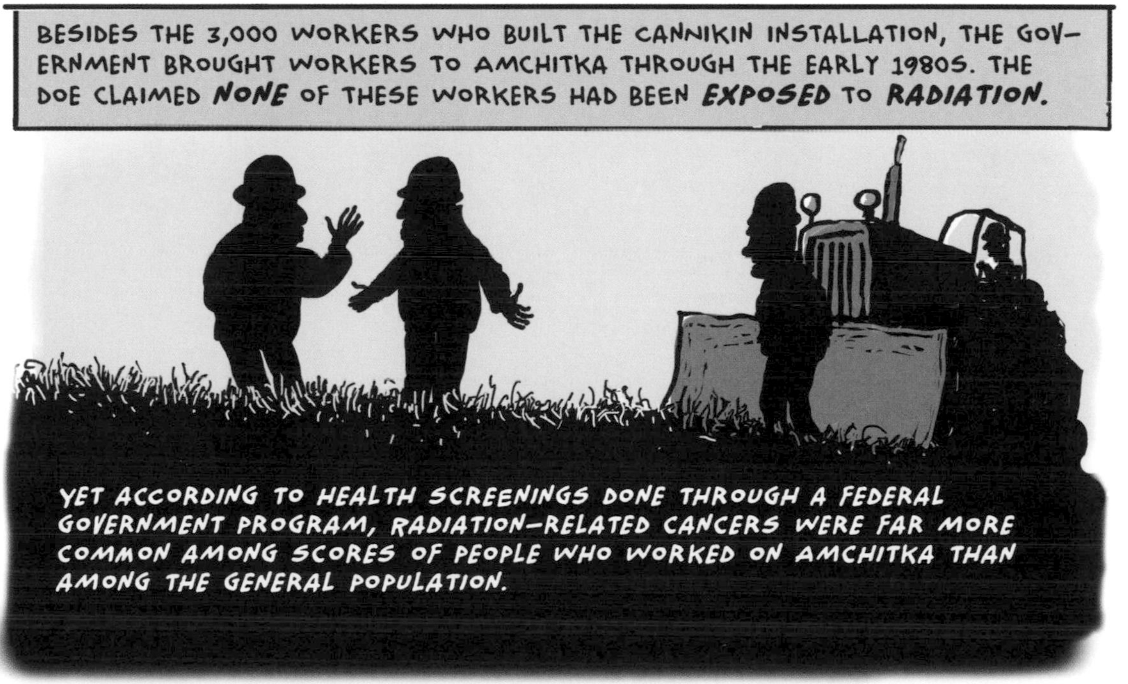
BESIDES THE 3,000 WORKERS WHO BUILT THE CANNIKIN INSTALLATION, THE GOVERNMENT BROUGHT WORKERS TO AMCHITKA THROUGH THE EARLY 1980S. THE DOE CLAIMED ***NONE*** OF THESE WORKERS HAD BEEN ***EXPOSED*** TO ***RADIATION.***
YET ACCORDING TO HEALTH SCREENINGS DONE THROUGH A FEDERAL GOVERNMENT PROGRAM, RADIATION-RELATED CANCERS WERE FAR MORE COMMON AMONG SCORES OF PEOPLE WHO WORKED ON AMCHITKA THAN AMONG THE GENERAL POPULATION.

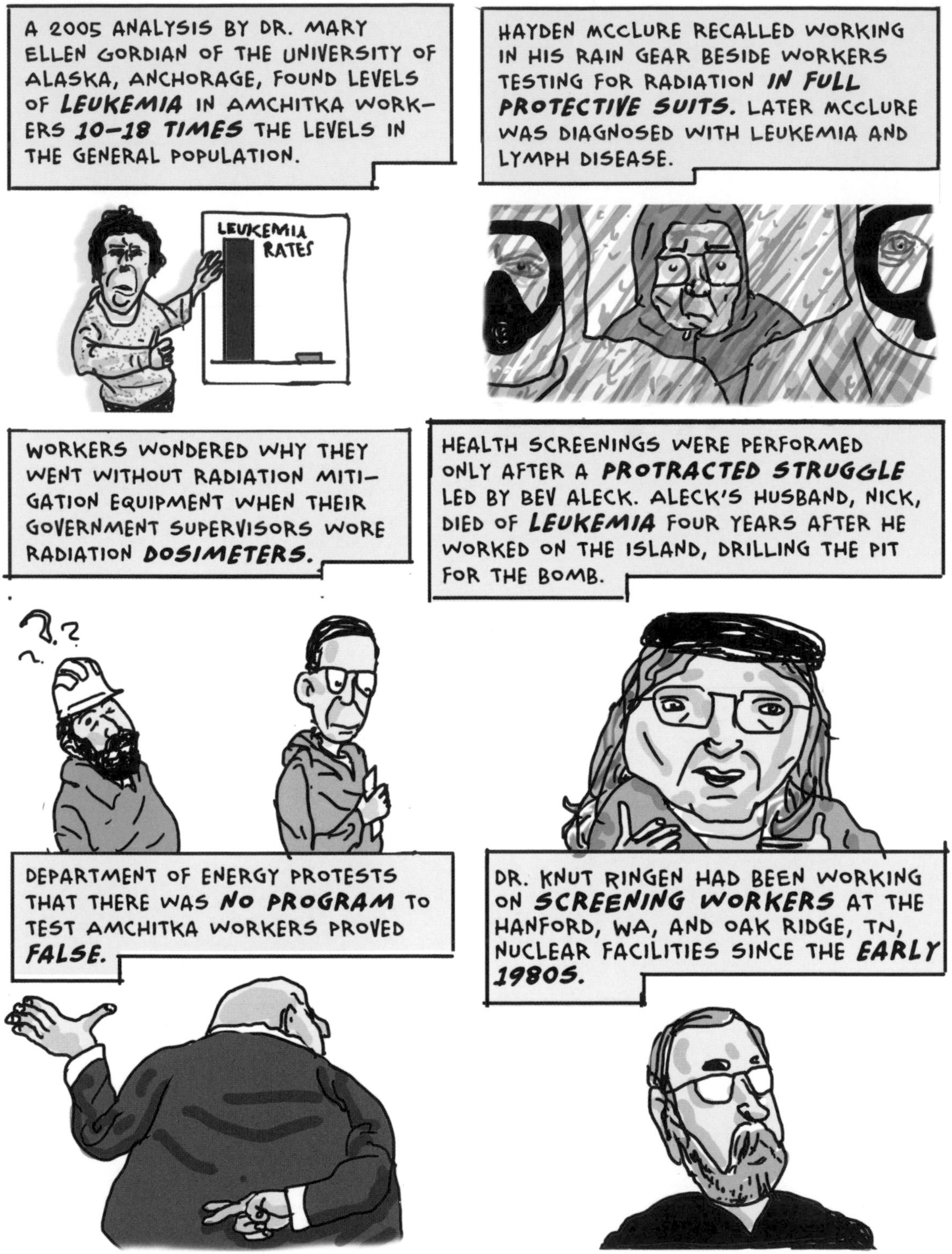
A 2005 ANALYSIS BY DR. MARY ELLEN GORDIAN OF THE UNIVERSITY OF ALASKA, ANCHORAGE, FOUND LEVELS OF LEUKEMIA IN AMCHITKA WORKERS 10–18 TIMES THE LEVELS IN THE GENERAL POPULATION.
LEUKEMIA RATES
HAYDEN MCCLURE RECALLED WORKING IN HIS RAIN GEAR BESIDE WORKERS TESTING FOR RADIATION IN FULL PROTECTIVE SUITS. LATER MCCLURE WAS DIAGNOSED WITH LEUKEMIA AND LYMPH DISEASE.
WORKERS WONDERED WHY THEY WENT WITHOUT RADIATION MITIGATION EQUIPMENT WHEN THEIR GOVERNMENT SUPERVISORS WORE RADIATION DOSIMETERS.
?.?
HEALTH SCREENINGS WERE PERFORMED ONLY AFTER A PROTRACTED STRUGGLE LED BY BEV ALECK. ALECK'S HUSBAND, NICK, DIED OF LEUKEMIA FOUR YEARS AFTER HE WORKED ON THE ISLAND, DRILLING THE PIT FOR THE BOMB.
DEPARTMENT OF ENERGY PROTESTS THAT THERE WAS NO PROGRAM TO TEST AMCHITKA WORKERS PROVED FALSE.
DR. KNUT RINGEN HAD BEEN WORKING ON SCREENING WORKERS AT THE HANFORD, WA, AND OAK RIDGE, TN, NUCLEAR FACILITIES SINCE THE EARLY 1980S.

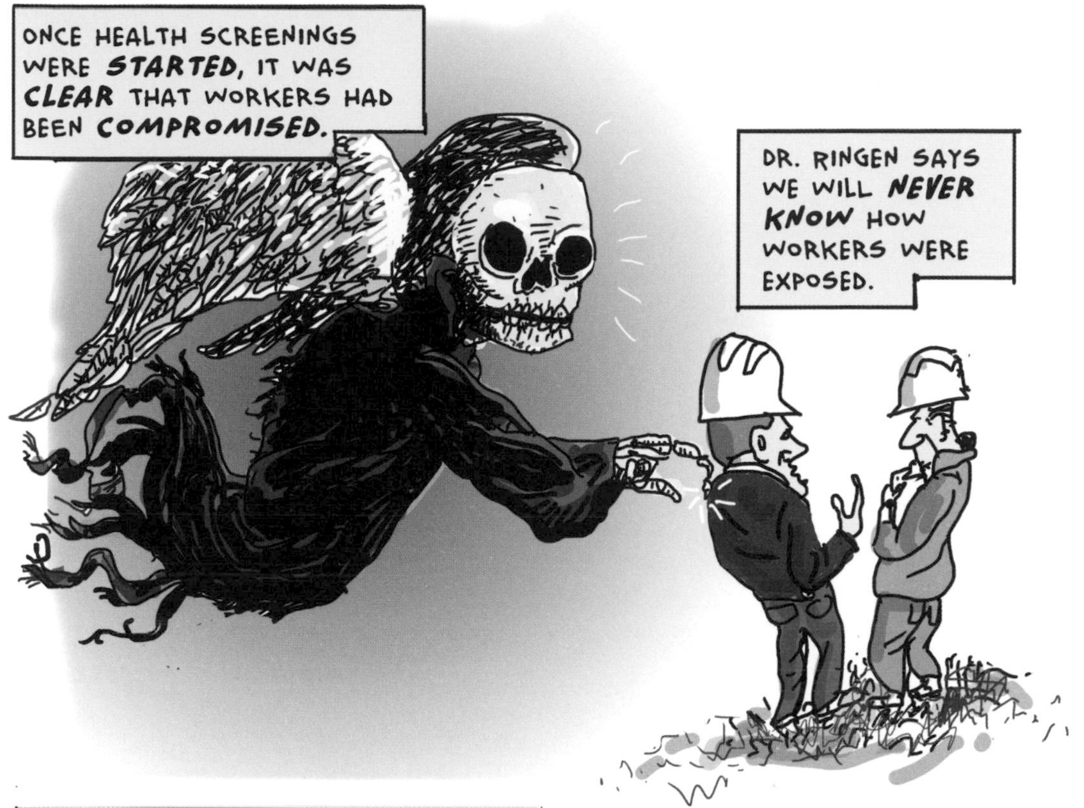
ONCE HEALTH SCREENINGS WERE **STARTED**, IT WAS **CLEAR** THAT WORKERS HAD BEEN **COMPROMISED.**
DR. RINGEN SAYS WE WILL **NEVER KNOW** HOW WORKERS WERE EXPOSED.

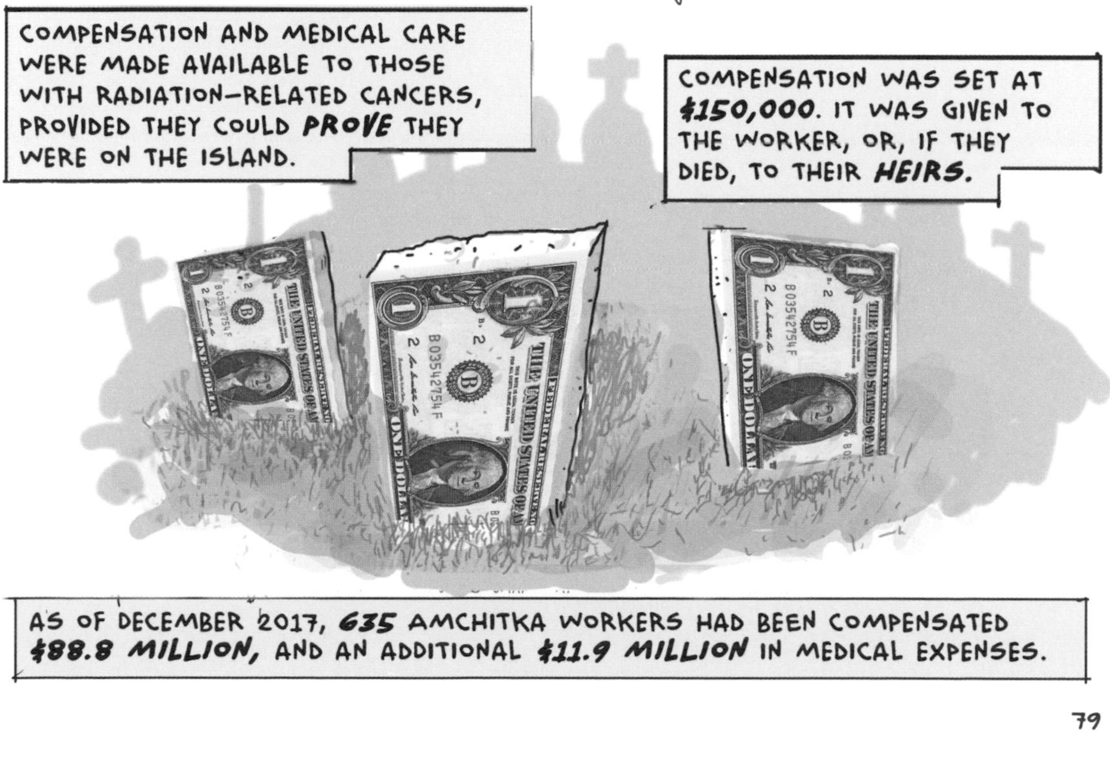
COMPENSATION AND MEDICAL CARE WERE MADE AVAILABLE TO THOSE WITH RADIATION-RELATED CANCERS, PROVIDED THEY COULD **PROVE** THEY WERE ON THE ISLAND.
COMPENSATION WAS SET AT **$150,000**. IT WAS GIVEN TO THE WORKER, OR, IF THEY DIED, TO THEIR **HEIRS.**
AS OF DECEMBER 2017, **635** AMCHITKA WORKERS HAD BEEN COMPENSATED **$88.8 MILLION,** AND AN ADDITIONAL **$11.9 MILLION** IN MEDICAL EXPENSES.

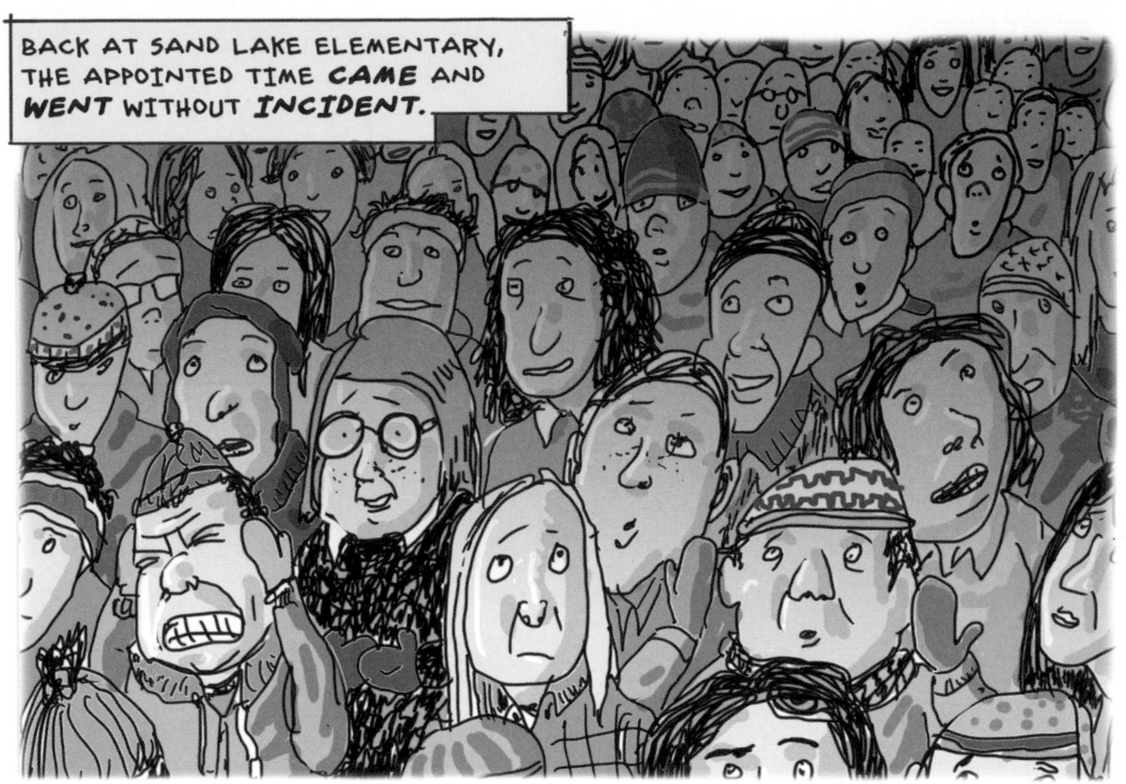
BACK AT SAND LAKE ELEMENTARY, THE APPOINTED TIME CAME AND WENT WITHOUT INCIDENT.

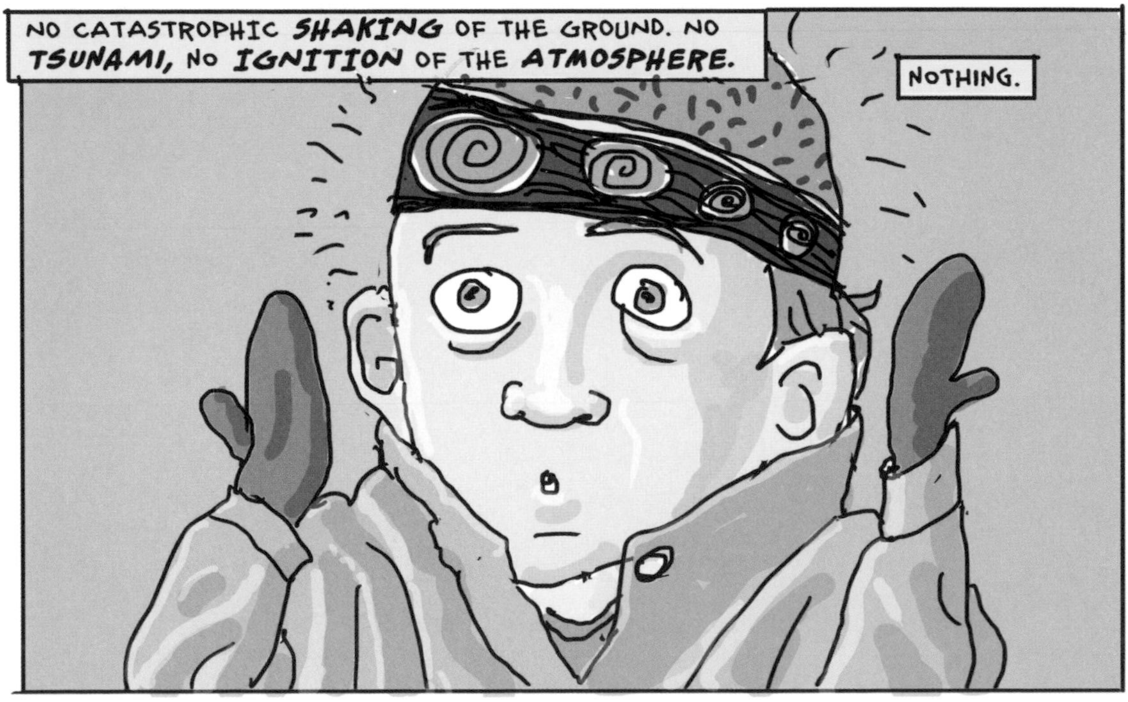
NO CATASTROPHIC SHAKING OF THE GROUND. NO TSUNAMI, NO IGNITION OF THE ATMOSPHERE.
NOTHING.

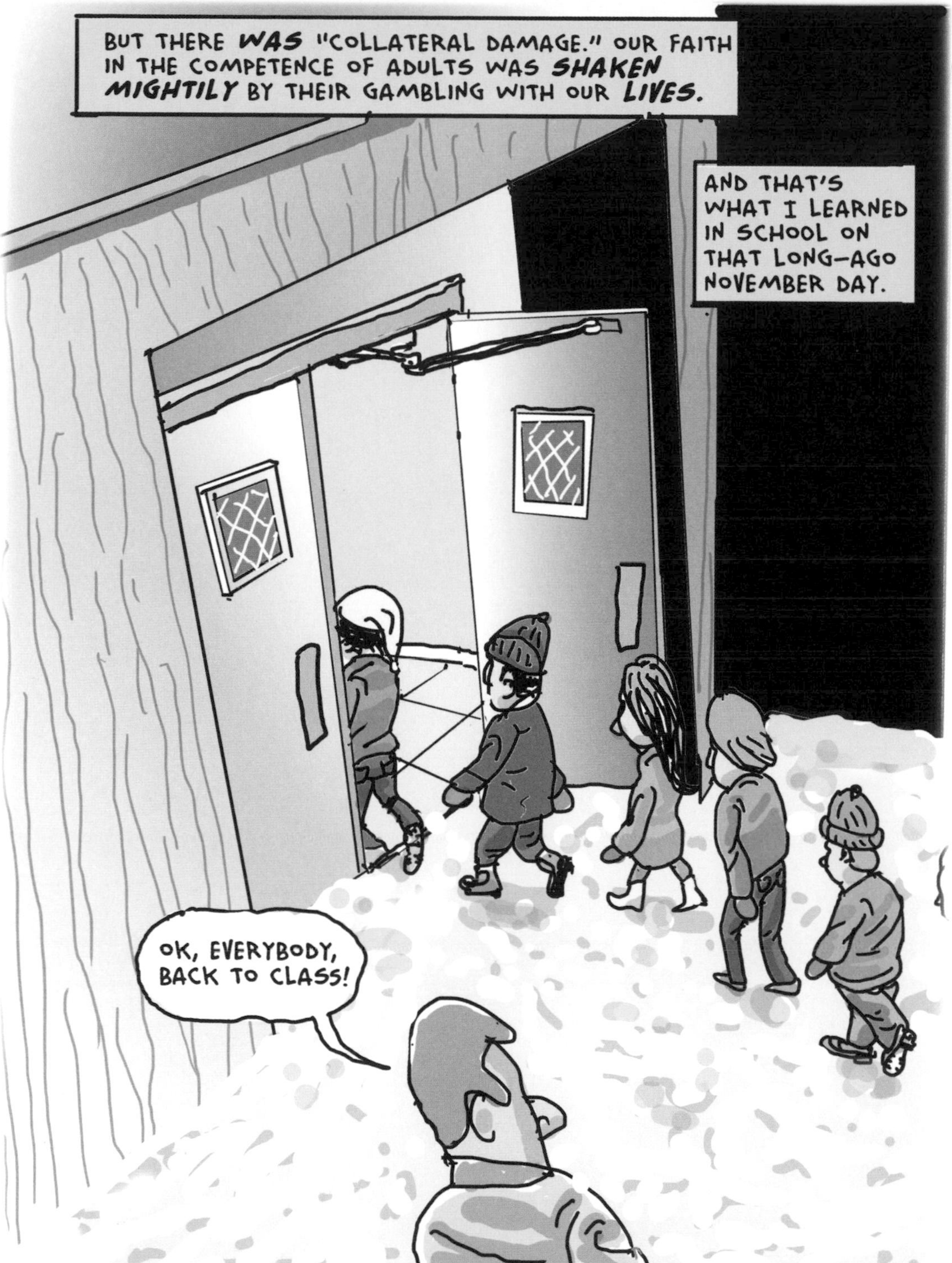
BUT THERE WAS "COLLATERAL DAMAGE." OUR FAITH IN THE COMPETENCE OF ADULTS WAS SHAKEN MIGHTILY BY THEIR GAMBLING WITH OUR LIVES.
AND THAT'S WHAT I LEARNED IN SCHOOL ON THAT LONG-AGO NOVEMBER DAY.
OK, EVERYBODY, BACK TO CLASS!

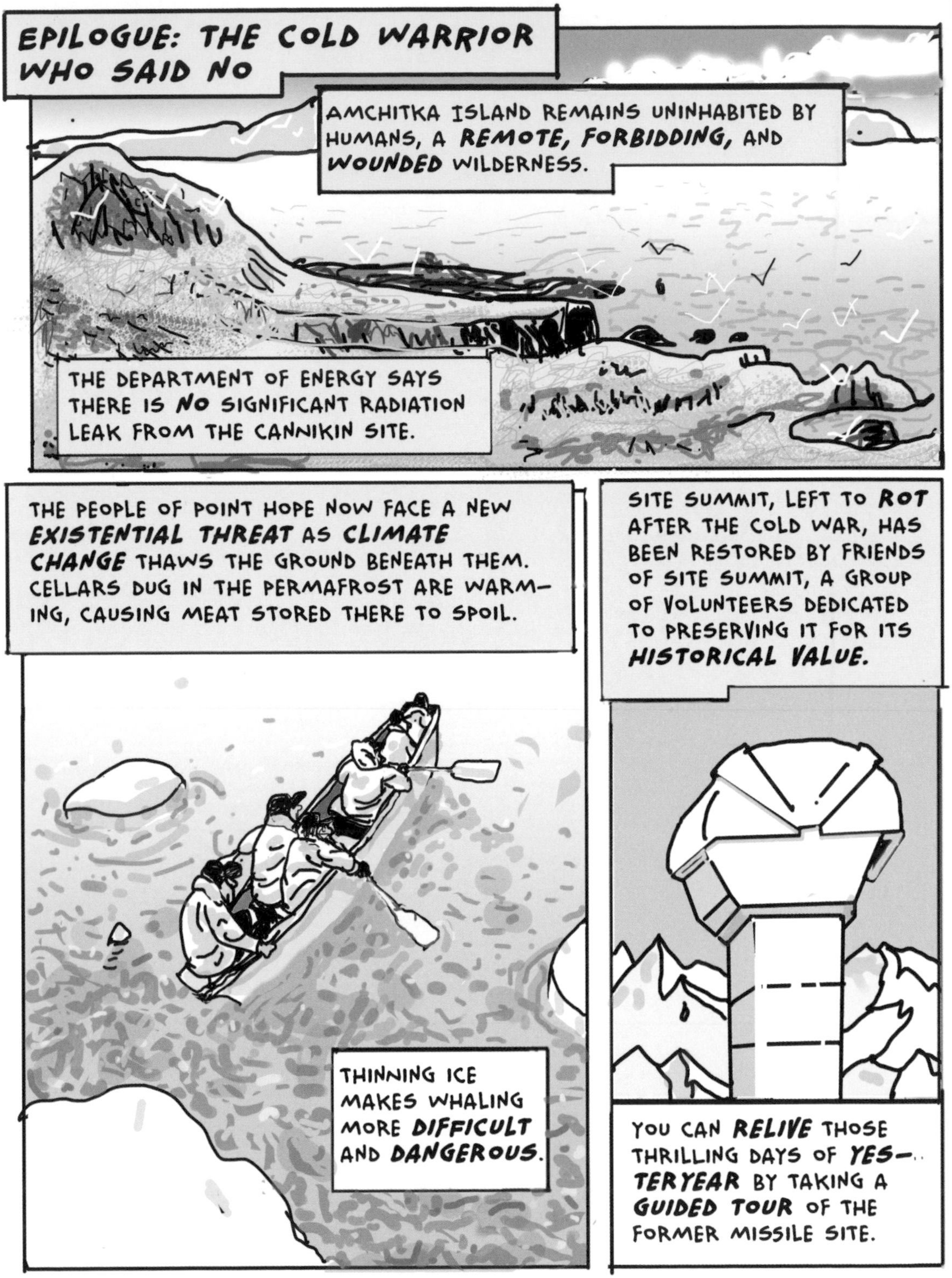
EPILOGUE: THE COLD WARRIOR WHO SAID NO
AMCHITKA ISLAND REMAINS UNINHABITED BY HUMANS, A REMOTE, FORBIDDING, AND WOUNDED WILDERNESS.
THE DEPARTMENT OF ENERGY SAYS THERE IS NO SIGNIFICANT RADIATION LEAK FROM THE CANNIKIN SITE.
THE PEOPLE OF POINT HOPE NOW FACE A NEW EXISTENTIAL THREAT AS CLIMATE CHANGE THAWS THE GROUND BENEATH THEM. CELLARS DUG IN THE PERMAFROST ARE WARMING, CAUSING MEAT STORED THERE TO SPOIL.
THINNING ICE MAKES WHALING MORE DIFFICULT AND DANGEROUS.
SITE SUMMIT, LEFT TO ROT AFTER THE COLD WAR, HAS BEEN RESTORED BY FRIENDS OF SITE SUMMIT, A GROUP OF VOLUNTEERS DEDICATED TO PRESERVING IT FOR ITS HISTORICAL VALUE.
YOU CAN RELIVE THOSE THRILLING DAYS OF YESTERYEAR BY TAKING A GUIDED TOUR OF THE FORMER MISSILE SITE.

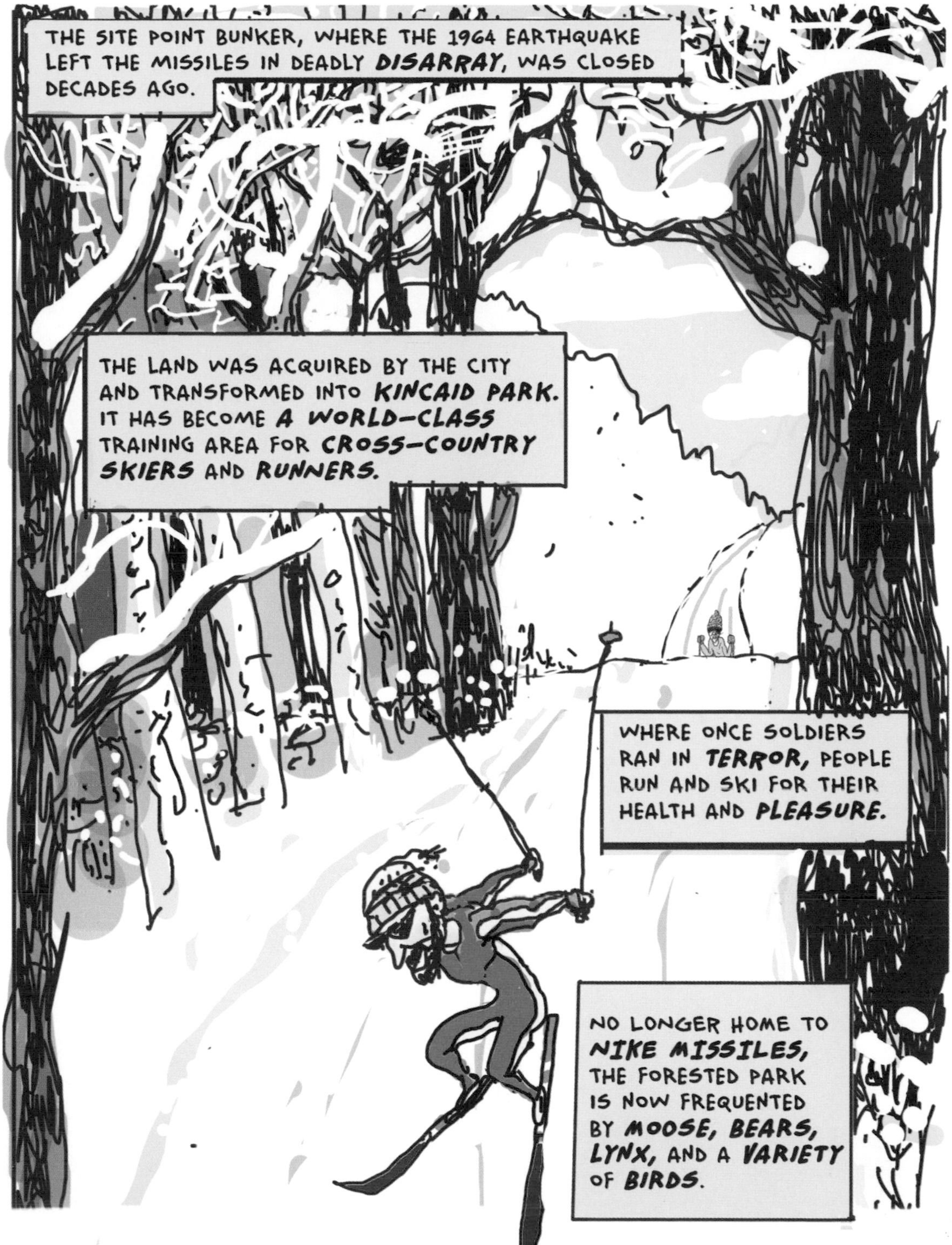
THE SITE POINT BUNKER, WHERE THE 1964 EARTHQUAKE LEFT THE MISSILES IN DEADLY DISARRAY, WAS CLOSED DECADES AGO.
THE LAND WAS ACQUIRED BY THE CITY AND TRANSFORMED INTO KINCAID PARK. IT HAS BECOME A WORLD-CLASS TRAINING AREA FOR CROSS-COUNTRY SKIERS AND RUNNERS.
WHERE ONCE SOLDIERS RAN IN TERROR, PEOPLE RUN AND SKI FOR THEIR HEALTH AND PLEASURE.
NO LONGER HOME TO NIKE MISSILES, THE FORESTED PARK IS NOW FREQUENTED BY MOOSE, BEARS, LYNX, AND A VARIETY OF BIRDS.

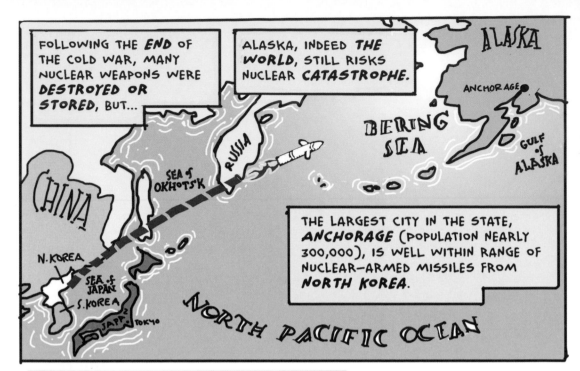

FOLLOWING THE *END* OF THE COLD WAR, MANY NUCLEAR WEAPONS WERE *DESTROYED OR STORED*, BUT...

ALASKA, INDEED *THE WORLD*, STILL RISKS NUCLEAR *CATASTROPHE.*

ALASKA

ANCHORAGE

BERING SEA

GULF of ALASKA

RUSSIA

SEA of OKHOTSK

CHINA

N. KOREA

SEA of JAPAN

S. KOREA

JAPAN TOKYO

THE LARGEST CITY IN THE STATE, *ANCHORAGE* (POPULATION NEARLY 300,000), IS WELL WITHIN RANGE OF NUCLEAR-ARMED MISSILES FROM *NORTH KOREA.*

NORTH PACIFIC OCEAN

APPROXIMATELY 90 PERCENT OF ALL NUCLEAR WARHEADS ARE OWNED BY RUSSIA AND THE UNITED STATES. THEY BOTH HAVE AROUND 4,000 WARHEADS IN THEIR MILITARY STOCK-PILES. CHINA HAS 350. NORTH KOREA IS BE-LIEVED TO HAVE 45 WARHEADS, INDIA AND PA-KISTAN AROUND 100 EACH, ISRAEL BETWEEN 20 AND 400. FRANCE HAS 290, AND THE U.K. 225.

MEANWHILE THE *LEADERSHIP* OF THE NUCLEAR-ARMED NATIONS HASN'T IMPROVED GREATLY SINCE *NIXON.*

WHERE DO WE FIND THE *COURAGE* TO FACE THIS PREDICAMENT? THE ANSWER LIES BENEATH THE WAVES OF *THE SARGASSO SEA*, WHERE A SINGLE SOVIET SUBMARINE OFFICER STOOD BETWEEN THE *WORLD* AND *DISASTER.*

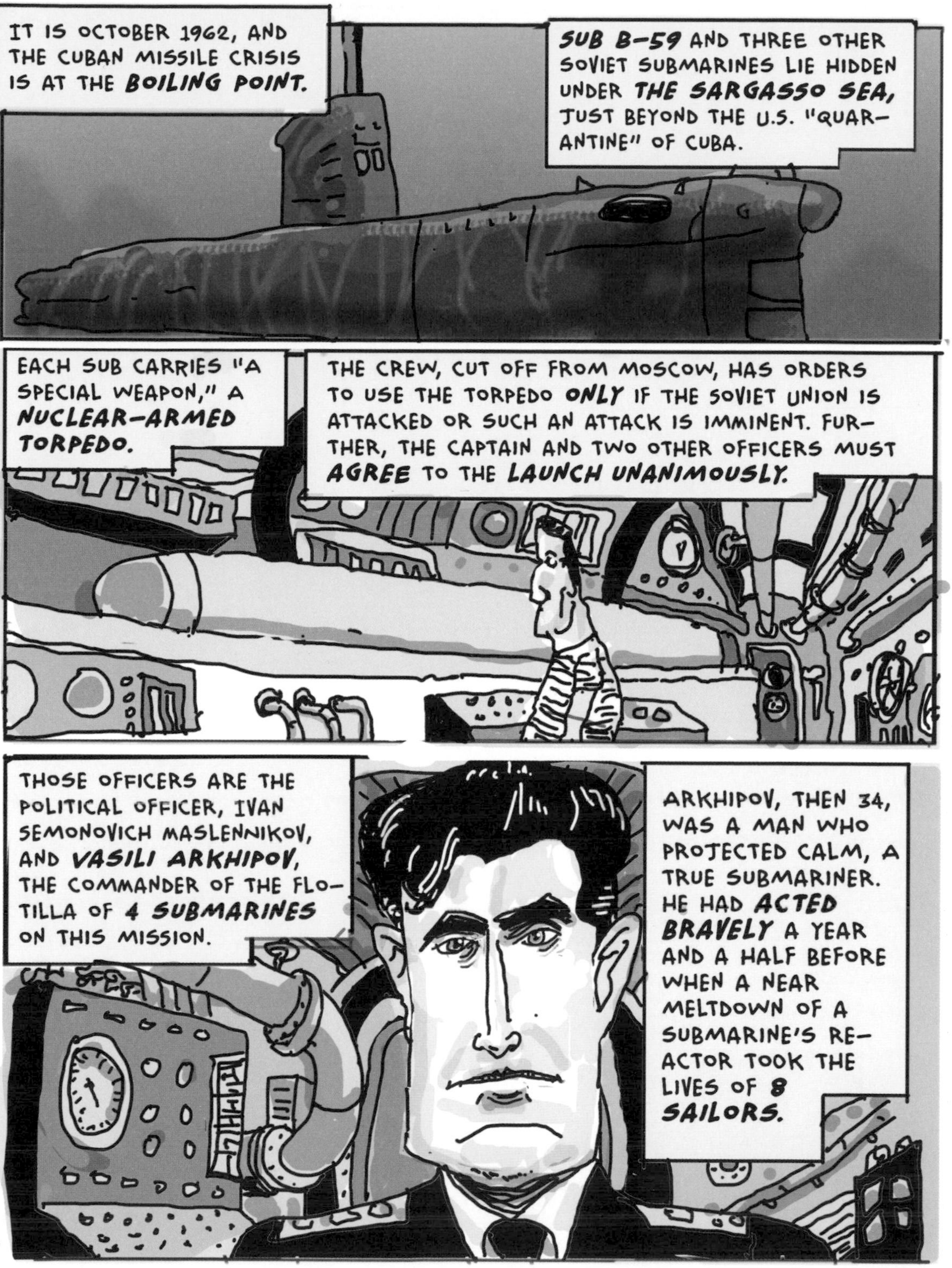
IT IS OCTOBER 1962, AND THE CUBAN MISSILE CRISIS IS AT THE BOILING POINT.
SUB B-59 AND THREE OTHER SOVIET SUBMARINES LIE HIDDEN UNDER THE SARGASSO SEA, JUST BEYOND THE U.S. "QUARANTINE" OF CUBA.
EACH SUB CARRIES "A SPECIAL WEAPON," A NUCLEAR-ARMED TORPEDO.
THE CREW, CUT OFF FROM MOSCOW, HAS ORDERS TO USE THE TORPEDO ONLY IF THE SOVIET UNION IS ATTACKED OR SUCH AN ATTACK IS IMMINENT. FURTHER, THE CAPTAIN AND TWO OTHER OFFICERS MUST AGREE TO THE LAUNCH UNANIMOUSLY.
THOSE OFFICERS ARE THE POLITICAL OFFICER, IVAN SEMONOVICH MASLENNIKOV, AND VASILI ARKHIPOV, THE COMMANDER OF THE FLOTILLA OF 4 SUBMARINES ON THIS MISSION.
ARKHIPOV, THEN 34, WAS A MAN WHO PROJECTED CALM, A TRUE SUBMARINER. HE HAD ACTED BRAVELY A YEAR AND A HALF BEFORE WHEN A NEAR MELTDOWN OF A SUBMARINE'S REACTOR TOOK THE LIVES OF 8 SAILORS.

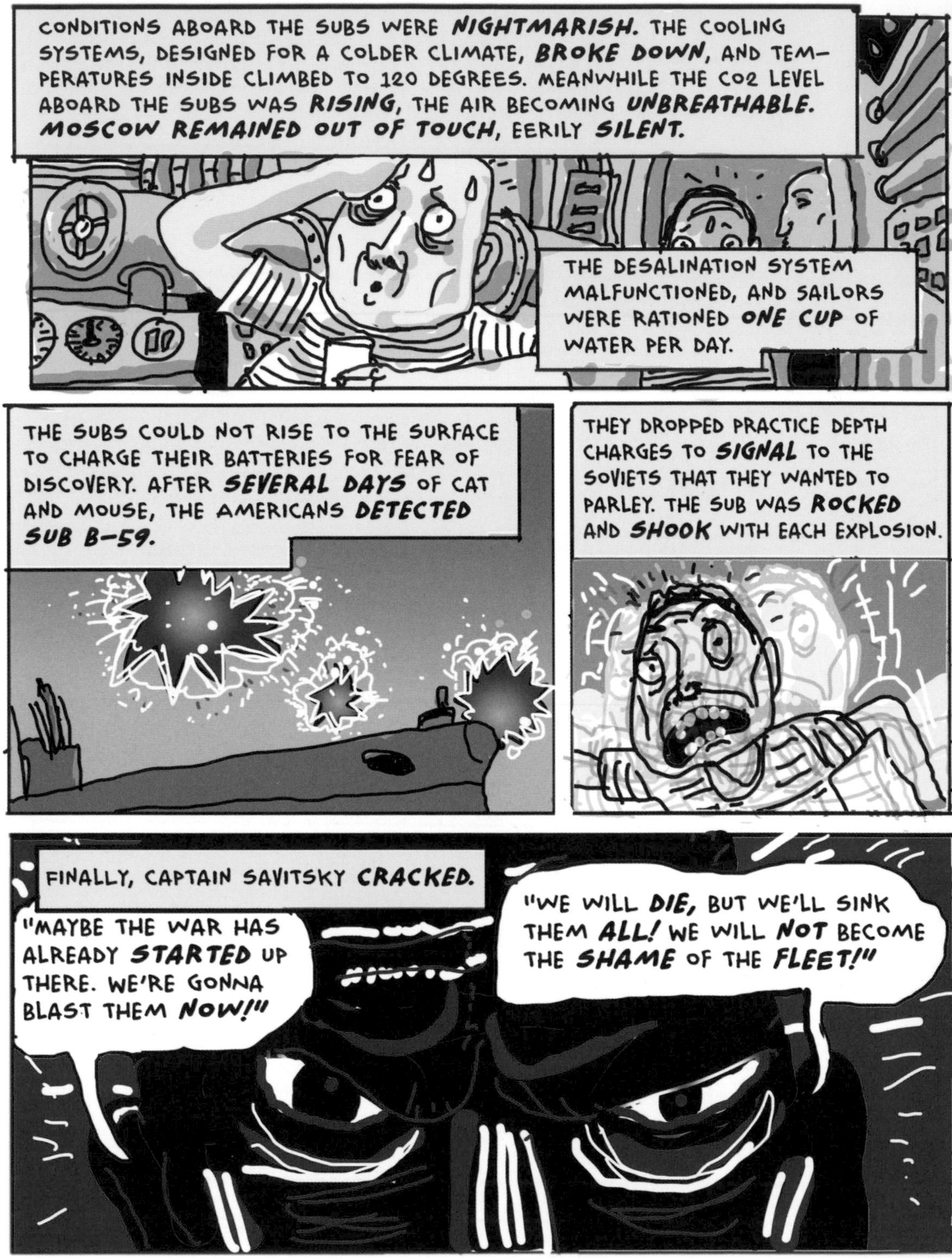
CONDITIONS ABOARD THE SUBS WERE NIGHTMARISH. THE COOLING SYSTEMS, DESIGNED FOR A COLDER CLIMATE, BROKE DOWN, AND TEMPERATURES INSIDE CLIMBED TO 120 DEGREES. MEANWHILE THE CO2 LEVEL ABOARD THE SUBS WAS RISING, THE AIR BECOMING UNBREATHABLE. MOSCOW REMAINED OUT OF TOUCH, EERILY SILENT.
THE DESALINATION SYSTEM MALFUNCTIONED, AND SAILORS WERE RATIONED ONE CUP OF WATER PER DAY.
THE SUBS COULD NOT RISE TO THE SURFACE TO CHARGE THEIR BATTERIES FOR FEAR OF DISCOVERY. AFTER SEVERAL DAYS OF CAT AND MOUSE, THE AMERICANS DETECTED SUB B-59.
THEY DROPPED PRACTICE DEPTH CHARGES TO SIGNAL TO THE SOVIETS THAT THEY WANTED TO PARLEY. THE SUB WAS ROCKED AND SHOOK WITH EACH EXPLOSION.
FINALLY, CAPTAIN SAVITSKY CRACKED.
"MAYBE THE WAR HAS ALREADY STARTED UP THERE. WE'RE GONNA BLAST THEM NOW!"
"WE WILL DIE, BUT WE'LL SINK THEM ALL! WE WILL NOT BECOME THE SHAME OF THE FLEET!"

ON SATURDAY, OCTOBER 27, 1962, AT 5 P.M. EASTERN DAYLIGHT TIME (EDT), SAVITSKY GAVE THE ORDER TO LOAD AND PREPARE TO FIRE THE NUCLEAR-ARMED TORPEDO AT A FLEET OF *U.S. NAVY VESSELS.*

ONE THING VARIOUS ACCOUNTS AGREE ON: FIRING THE NUCLEAR TORPEDO WOULD LIKELY HAVE PRECIPITATED WORLD WAR III, A *GLOBAL THERMONUCLEAR WAR.*

SAVITSKY AND THE POLITICAL OFFICER, IVAN SEMONOVICH MASLENNIKOV, *AGREED TO LAUNCH.* THE ONLY MAN WHO STOOD IN THE WAY OF A *NUCLEAR DISASTER* WAS *VASILI ARKHIPOV.*

AN ARGUMENT FOLLOWED, AND WE DO NOT KNOW *WHAT* WAS SAID. BUT IT IS LIKELY THAT ARKHIPOV WAS ABLE TO CONVINCE SAVITSKY THAT THE BOMBARDMENT FROM THE DEPTH CHARGES WAS THE AMERICANS' SIGNAL *TO TALK.*

I DO NOT AGREE.

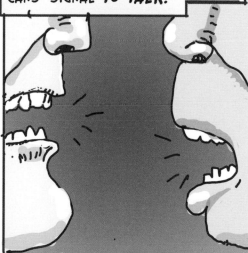

AS HISTORIAN MARTIN J. SHERWIN NOTES, WHILE THE WORLD THOUGHT KHRUSCHEV AND KENNEDY HELD THE FATE OF THE *GLOBE* IN THEIR HANDS, THE FUTURE WAS BEING DETERMINED BY TWO *SOVIET SUBMARINERS.*

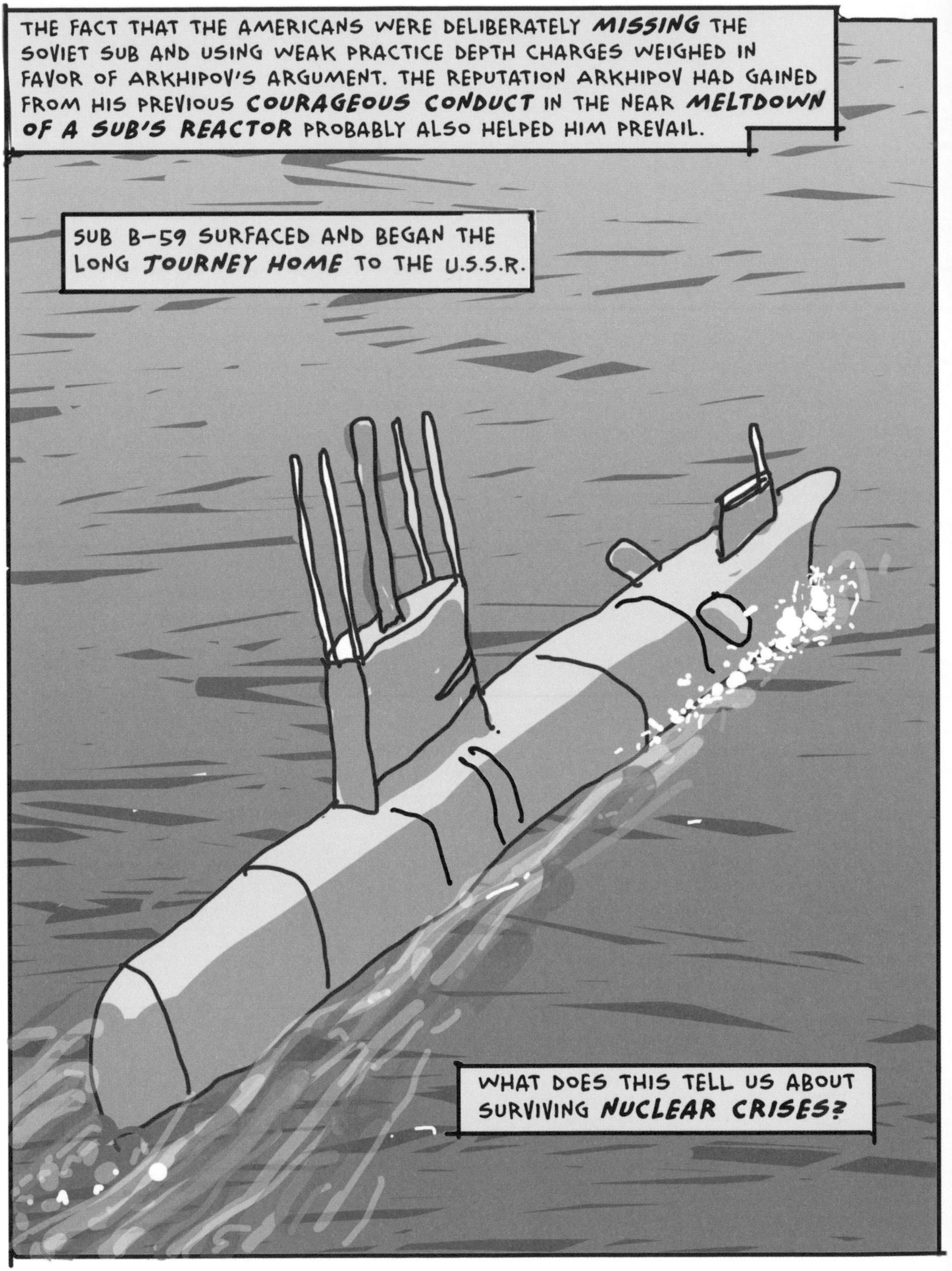
THE FACT THAT THE AMERICANS WERE DELIBERATELY ***MISSING*** THE SOVIET SUB AND USING WEAK PRACTICE DEPTH CHARGES WEIGHED IN FAVOR OF ARKHIPOV'S ARGUMENT. THE REPUTATION ARKHIPOV HAD GAINED FROM HIS PREVIOUS ***COURAGEOUS CONDUCT*** IN THE NEAR ***MELTDOWN OF A SUB'S REACTOR*** PROBABLY ALSO HELPED HIM PREVAIL.
SUB B-59 SURFACED AND BEGAN THE LONG ***JOURNEY HOME*** TO THE U.S.S.R.
WHAT DOES THIS TELL US ABOUT SURVIVING ***NUCLEAR CRISES?***

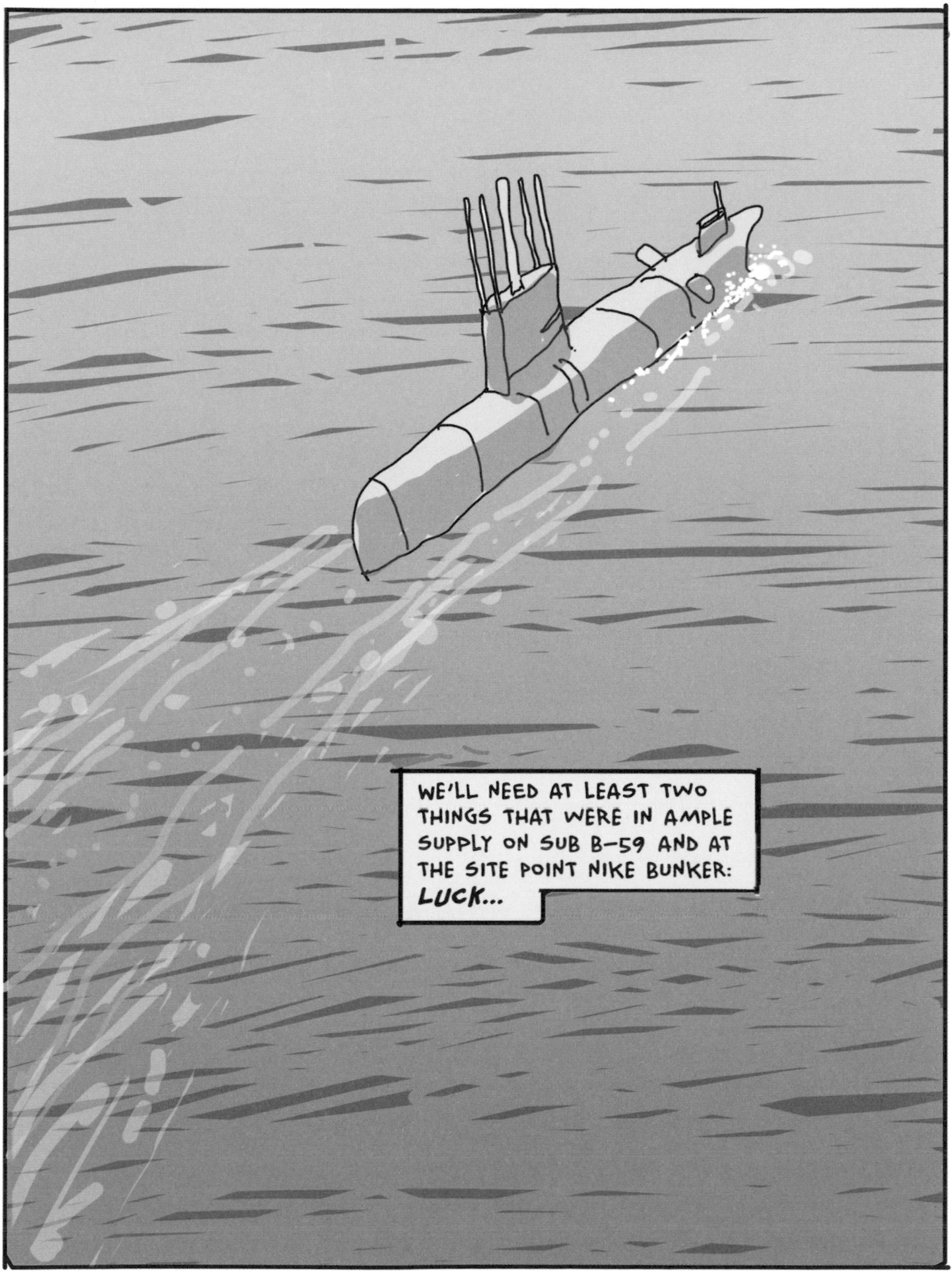
WE'LL NEED AT LEAST TWO THINGS THAT WERE IN AMPLE SUPPLY ON SUB B-59 AND AT THE SITE POINT NIKE BUNKER: **LUCK...**

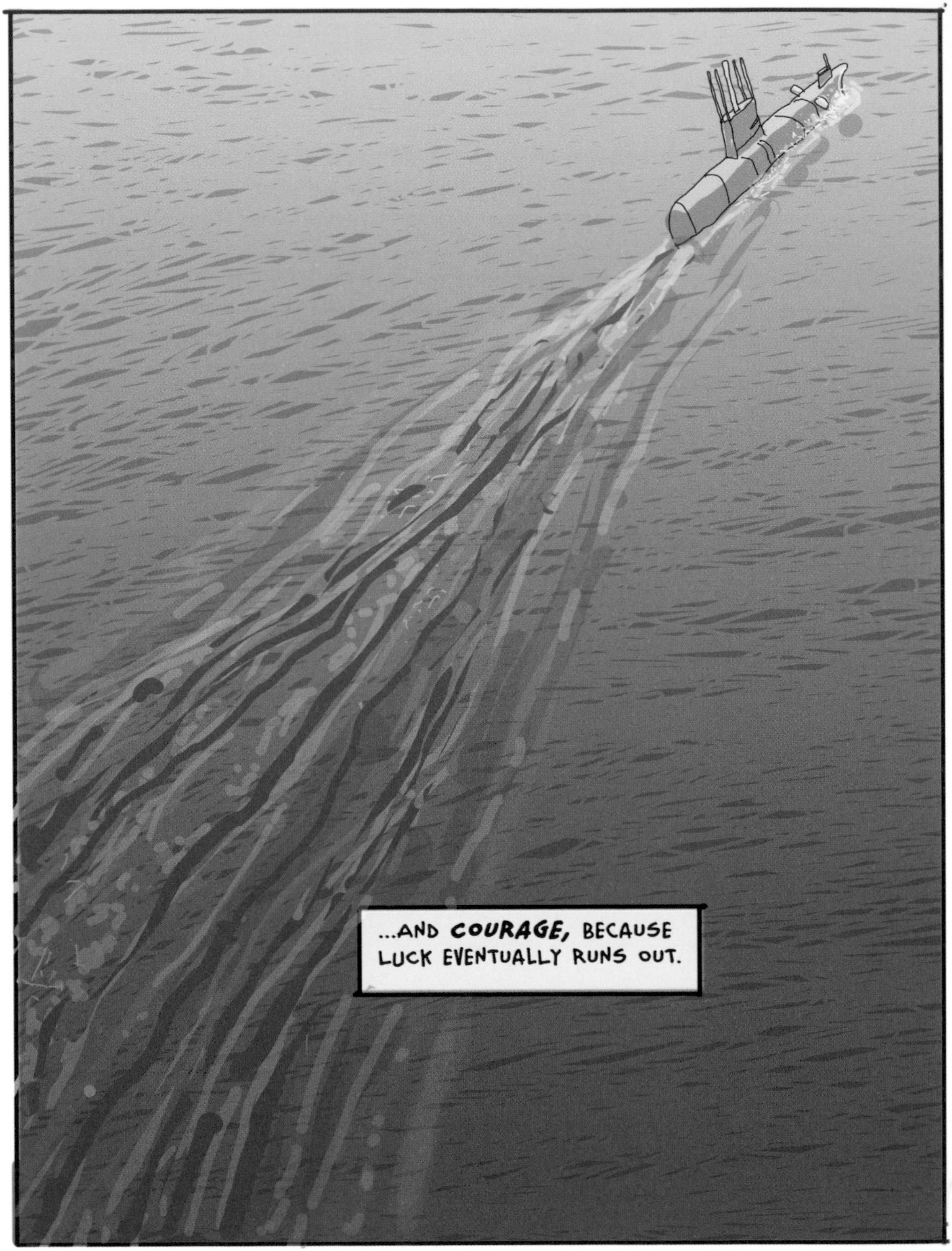
...AND **COURAGE,** BECAUSE LUCK EVENTUALLY RUNS OUT.

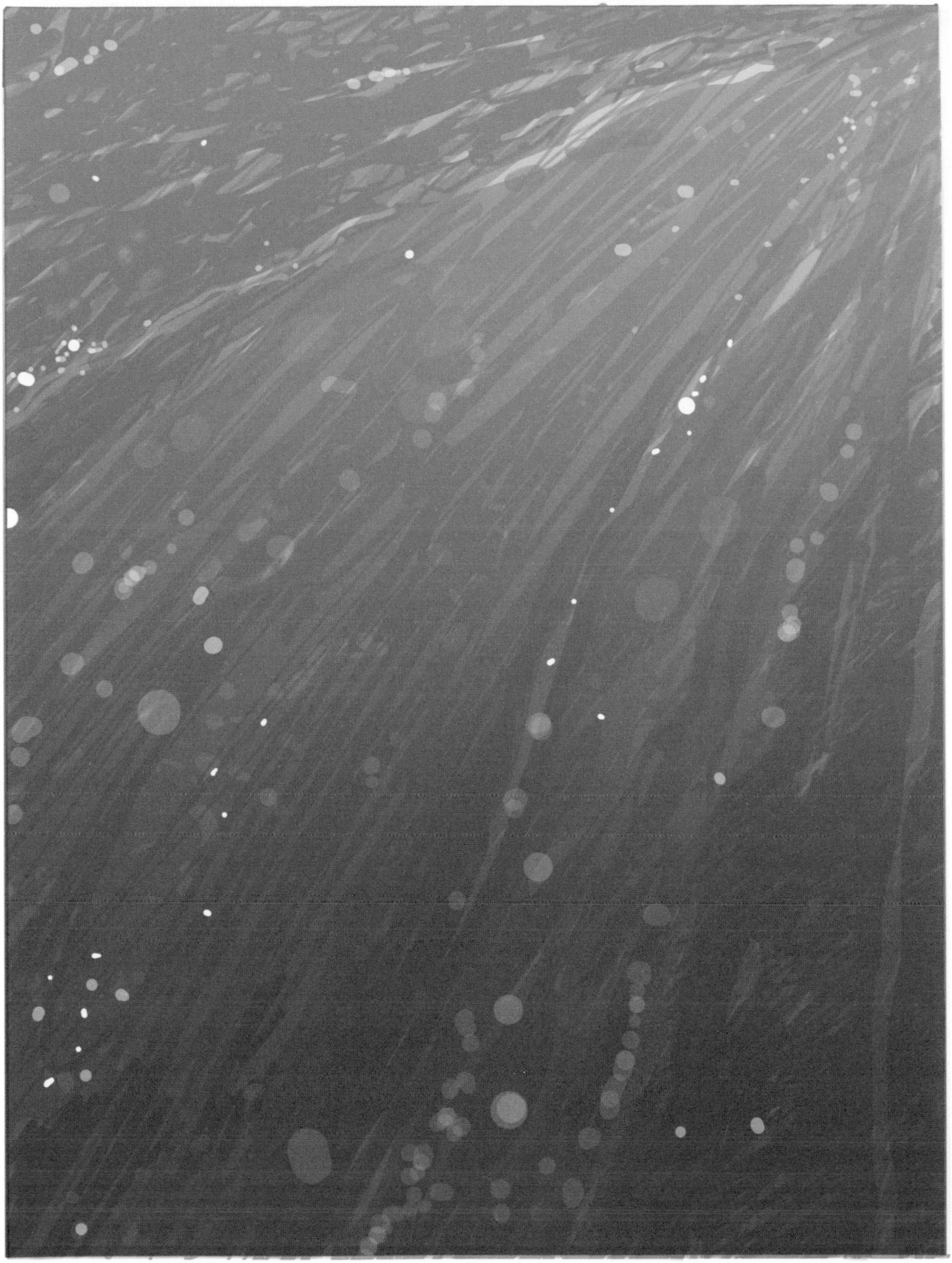

NOTES

Pages 1–5, 7: Walter Isaacson, "Chain Reaction: From Einstein to the Atomic Bomb," *Discover*, March 17, 2008, https://www .discovermagazine.com/the-sciences/chain -reaction-from-einstein-to-the-atomic-bomb.

Page 3: Bounty on Einstein's head, Einstein "not yet hanged": Britannica, "Albert Einstein," https://www.britannica.com/biography/Albert -Einstein/Nazi-backlash-and-coming-to -America.

Page 4: U.S. Department of Energy, The Manhattan Project: An Interactive History, "Einstein's Letter to Roosevelt," https://www .osti.gov/opennet/manhattan-project-history /Resources/einstein_letter_photograph.htm.

Page 7: "Famous Diary Entries: Einstein Confesses His 'One Great Mistake," *Endpaper* (blog), March 25, 2013, http://blog.paperblanks .com/2013/03/famous-diary-entries-einstein -confesses-his-one-great-mistake/.

Page 15: Benjamin Schwarz, "The Real Cuban Missile Crisis," *Atlantic Monthly*, January/ February 2013, https://www.theatlantic.com /magazine/archive/2013/01/the-real-cuban -missile-crisis/309190/.

Pages 17–20: Tour of Site Summit, interview with Jim Renkert (Friends of Nike Summit).

Page 18: "Nike Hercules," Wikipedia, https://en .wikipedia.org/wiki/Nike_Hercules; The Nike Historical Society, "Hercules MIM-14, MIM-14A, MIM-14B," https://nikemissile.org/IFC /nike_hercules.shtml.

Page 22: Number of Alaskan earthquake deaths: Alaska Division of Public Health, Health Analytics and Vital Records, "Alaska

Facts and Figures: 1964 Earthquake Mortality in Alaska," https://health.alaska.gov/dph /VitalStats/Documents/PDFs/AK_1964_EQ _082219.pdf.

Page 23: NikeAlaska.org, "Site Point, Alaska: The Last AADCP of the Last Operational U.S. Nike-Hercules Missile Battalion," http://nikealaska.org/AADCP /AADCP.html.

Page 24: https://www.businessinsider .com, http://ed-thelan.org.

Page 25: Soldiers panic, run: NikeAlaska. org, "Site Point, Alaska."

Page 26: Project Jukebox, Digital Branch of the University of Alaska Fairbanks Oral History Program, video interview with George Wallot: https://jukebox.uaf.edu /interviews/2448.

Page 27: NikeAlaska.org.

Page 32: Teller plays Bach on piano: Freeman Dyson, *Disturbing the Universe* (New York: HarperCollins, 1979); Dr. Strangelove, involvement in Manhattan Project: Joel N. Shurkin, "Edward Teller, 'Father of the Hydrogen Bomb,' Is Dead at 95," https://news.stanford.edu/news/2003 /september24/tellerobit-924.html; Teller background, "Father of H-bomb": Ashutosh Jogalekar, "The Many Tragedies of Edward Teller," *The Curious Wavefunction* (blog), *Scientific American*, January 15, 2014, https:// blogs.scientificamerican.com/the-curious -wavefunction/the-many-tragedies-of-edward -teller/; fear of setting the atmosphere afire: John Horgan, "Bethe, Teller, Trinity and the End of Earth," *Cross-Check* (blog), *Scientific*

American, August 4, 2015, https://blogs .scientificamerican.com/cross-check/bethe -teller-trinity-and-the-end-of-earth/.

Page 33: Manhattan Project priorities, squabbles, reaction of Teller to first atomic bomb explosion: Shurkin, "Edward Teller"; J. Robert Oppenheimer, "Now I am become Death" (video), https://www.youtube.com /watch?v=lb13ynu3Iac.

Page 34: Shurkin, "Edward Teller"; Ulam corrected Teller's design of H-bomb: NPR, "Another Father of the Hydrogen Bomb," April 4, 2009, https://www.npr.org/templates /story/story.php?storyId=102748024; Teller and asteroids: Timothy Ferris, "Is This the End?," *New Yorker*, January 27, 1997, https:// www.newyorker.com/magazine/1997/01/27 /is-this-the-end; instant harbor idea, locating Project Chariot in Alaska: Ed Regis, "What Could Go Wrong?," Slate, September 30, 2015, https://slate.com/technology/2015/09/project -plowshare-the-1950s-plan-to-use-nukes-to -make-roads-and-redirect-rivers.html/.

Page 35: Simi Press, "The Firecracker Boys," *Medium*, May 28, 2020, https://medium.com /write-and-review/the-firecracker-boys -b58609b6f65; labeling of the Project Chariot advocates as the "Firecracker Boys": Dan O'Neill, *The Firecracker Boys* (New York: Basic Books, 1994), 74; layout of Project Chariot proposal: Suzanna Caldwell, "'Project Chariot' Brings Potential Nuclear Disaster Story Full- Circle," *Anchorage Daily News*, October 13, 2012 (updated September 28, 2016), https://adn.com /film-tv/article-project-chariot-brings-potential -nuclear-disaster-story-full-circle/2012/10/14.

Page 36: Point Hope the oldest continuously inhabited place in North America: Arctic Slope Native Association, "Point Hope," https://arcticslope.org/about/communities/point -hope/; Iñupiat were afterthoughts: O'Neill, *Firecracker Boys*, 115–16; Chariot advocates met with people in Anchorage, Fairbanks, and Juneau: ibid., 34; black diamonds will pay better than gold, objections about economic practicality of proposed harbor: ibid., 36; Teller claims to be open to other sites, ideas: ibid., 41.

Page 37: Withdrawal of land for Project Chariot: O'Neill, *Firecracker Boys*, 41; Teller dismisses fears of biologists: ibid., 39; Teller flatters Alaskans: ibid., 40; urban Alaska newspapers' support of Project Chariot: ibid., 41, 76; rationale shift to justify Project Chariot: ibid., 70–71.

Page 38: University of Alaska biologists' concerns about Project Chariot: ibid., 72–75; Committee for the Study of Atomic Testing in Alaska: ibid., 78–79 AEC says it will pursue Project Chariot elsewhere: ibid., 80; federal dollars to biologists: ibid., 90.

Page 39: Lies of Edward Teller: ibid., 49.

Page 40: Air blast would have damaged Point Hope: ibid., 48; Charlie Sokaitis, "Once Upon Alaska: Project Chariot," Alaska's News Source, February 7, 2020, https://www .alaskasnewssource.com/content/news/Once -Upon-Alaska-Project-Chariot-567659291 .html.

Page 41: Strontium and the human body, elevated levels of strontium-90 in cow's milk:

"The Baby Tooth Survey," *The Pauling Blog*, June 1, 2011, https://paulingblog.wordpress .com/2011/06/01/the-baby-tooth-survey/; strontium-90 in caribou, elevated levels in caribou consumers: Arthur R. Schulert, "Strontium-90 in Alaska," *Science* 136, no. 3511 (1962): 146–48, https://www.science.org/doi /pdf/10.1126/science.136.3511.146.

Page 42: Point Hope villagers grill AEC: O'Neill, *Firecracker Boys*, 136–38.

Page 43: Sophistication of Dan Lisburne: ibid., 116.

Page 44: Howard Rock, founding of *Tundra Times*: Lael Morgan, *Art and Eskimo Power: The Life and Times of Alaskan Howard Rock* (Kenmore WA: Epicenter Press 1998); Project Chariot officially ended: Sokaitis, "Once Upon Alaska."

Page 45: Alaska Indigenous people were inspired by success of Project Chariot opposition, carried momentum forward in quest for Native land rights, AEC contaminates test site to observe effects of radiation on Arctic environment: Thomas Brown, "Project Chariot: That Time the Government Tried to Nuke Alaska," *Alaska Native News*, August 3, 2018, https://alaska -native-news.com/project-chariot%E2%80%8A -%E2%80%8Athat-time-the-government-tried -to-nuke-alaska/36645/.

Page 46: Contaminated soil, vegetation, paraphernalia gathered into mound, site visited by elected officials: O'Neill, *Firecracker Boys*, 304, 308.

Page 47: Cleanup of waste mound, shipping contaminated material out of state: Douglas L. Vandegraft, "Project Chariot: Nuclear Legacy of Cape Thompson," http://thefrenchnuclearway.anegeo.org/ideologie/docsideologie/docs/Plowshare_Chariot_project.pdf.

Page 52: Alleged purpose of three explosions: "Cannikin," Wikipedia, https://en.wikipedia.org/wiki/Cannikin. University of Virginia Presidential Recordings Program.

Page 53: President Kennedy decries the "Soft American": "Read It Here: Kennedy's The Soft American," Recreating with Kids, http://recreatingwithkids.com/news/read-it-here-kennedys-the-soft-american.

Page 56: Founding of Greenpeace: Greenpeace International, "Amchitka: The Founding Voyage," Greenpeace website, May 14, 2007, https://www.greenpeace.org/international/story/46686/amchitka-the-founding-voyage/; "Choice on Amchitka," editorial, *New York Times*, August 2, 1971, https://www.nytimes.com/1971/08/02/archives/choice-on-amchitka/; Supreme Court involvement: "Cannikin," editorial, *New York Times*, November 6, 1971, https://www.nytimes.com/1971/11/06/archives/cannikin.html; federal agency objections covered up: Jeffrey St. Clair, "The Bomb That Cracked an Island," *CounterPunch*, September 27, 2013, https://www.counterpunch.org/2013/09/27/the-bomb-that-cracked-an-island/.

Page 57: Seven federal agencies asked to evaluate Cannikin test, only two supported it: "Choice on Amchitka."

Page 59–60: University of Virginia Presidential Recordings Library.

Page 74: Environmental effects: St. Clair, "Bomb That Cracked an Island."

Page 75: Video of ground heaving, trailers being tossed: "Cannikin Nuclear Test Footage," Military.com, January 19, 2012, https://www.military.com/video/nuclear-bombs/nuclear-weapons/cannikin-nuclear-test-footage/1402452751001.

Page 77: Greenpeace finds radioactive traces on Amchitka: Pam Miller, "Nuclear Flashback: The Return to Amchitka," Greenpeace report, https://arctichealth.org/en/viewer?file=%2fmedia%2fpubs%2f301210%2fNuclear_Flashback_1996.pdf#phrase=false1998.pdf; Greenpeace found no tritium, findings dismissed: David Perlman, "Blast from the Past," *SF Gate*, December 17, 2001, https://www.sfgate.com/news/article/blast-from-the-past-researchers-worry-that-2839679.php; workers were brought to Amchitka through early 1980s, DOE denies they were exposed to radiation, radiation-related cancers far more common among Amchitka workers compared to general population: Charles Wohlforth, "Why a Bomb Test in the Aleutians Still Strikes Fear in Workers 46 Years Later," *Anchorage Daily News*, January 28, 2017 (updated December 2, 2017), https://www.adn.com/opinions/2017/01/28/why-a-bomb-test-in-the-aleutians-still-strikes-fear-in-workers-46-years-later/.

Pages 77–79: Wohlforth, "Why a Bomb Test."

Page 84: Federation of American Scientists, "Status of World Nuclear Forces," https://fas.org/issues/nuclear-weapons/status-world-nuclear-forces/.

Page 85: Arkhipov's character: Robert Krulwich, "You and Almost Everyone You Know Owe Your Life to This Man," *Curiously Krulwich* (blog), National Geographic, March 25, 2016, https://www.nationalgeographic.com/culture/article/you-and-almost-everyone-you-know-owe-your-life-to-this-man; PBS, "The Man Who Saved the World," episode of *Secrets of the Dead*, October 12, 2012, https://www.pbs.org/wnet/secrets/the-man-who-saved-the-world-about-this-episode/871/.

Pages 86–87: Martin J. Sherwin, "The Cuban Missile Crisis Revisited: Nuclear Deterrence? Good Luck!," George Mason University College of Humanities and Social Sciences, July 16, 2012, https://chss.gmu.edu/articles/4198tt.

Pages 87–88: "Vasily Arkhipov," Wikipedia, https://en.wikipedia.org/wiki/Vasily_Arkhipov.

ACKNOWLEDGMENTS

Some of the material in this book appeared previously on the comics website The Nib; thanks to Matt Bors and Andy Warner for their advice and edits. Thanks also to Jim Renkert for his dedication to preserving Site Summit and for alerting me to the Site Point fiasco. The bulk of the information about Project Chariot was first reported by Dan O'Neill in his authoritative and damning book *The Firecracker Boys*. There is no better source of the story.